This 1929 picture links two main characters of this book with the missionary past in Africa. Twyla Ludwig and her son Charles, author of this book, pose with Matthew Wellington, the last surviving porter who carried David Livingstone's body from Ujiji to the coast.

Upper left: An elderly Kikuyu is shown with his decorated snuffbox and beard pluckers. Upper right: A Bunyore woman and her pipe. Below: Men of a Kenya village suck through beer sticks from a common pot.

MAMA Was a
MISSIONARY

By
Charles Ludwig

ZONDERVAN PUBLISHING HOUSE
GRAND RAPIDS   MICHIGAN

Library of Congress Catalog Card Number 77-133354

Zondervan paperback edition 1970
Second printing   1971

For Dad,
Who Cooperated

Printed in the United States of America

Upper left: "Mama" Ludwig prays for a little boy. Note his naval hernia, at the time much admired in his tribe. Upper right: This man got the nickname "Jiggers" after Dad Ludwig removed so many jiggers from his feet. Below: A tribal ceremonial in Kenya.

Top: A witch doctor prepares to pour blood from a sacrificed goat on the head of a little boy. This is supposed to keep the spirit of his dead mother from killing him. Below: The Ludwig family spent two of their early years in Kenya living in this mission station laundry.

MAMA WAS A MISSIONARY

1

We were just finishing our noon meal when a barefoot native cook burst into the dining room all out of breath. "Missi Ludwig-i," she exclaimed, her large brown eyes bright with excitement, "there's a woman outside dying in childbirth. You'd better hurry. The heathen are beating her with a club, and a big woman is holding her nose and blowing into her mouth. And the witch doctor . . ."

Without waiting for her to finish, Mother gulped down her last swallow of Simba Chai and headed for the kitchen. "Put some water on the stove, and get plenty of wood to heat some more when I need it," she ordered in clumsy Olinyore. Then, clapping her hands sharply to arouse the loitering servants, and focusing her brown eye and blue eye on them, she added fiercely, "And don't run off!"

She jammed a thick cork helmet on her mass of long, curly brown hair and strode out into the yard with short, determined steps, her small artistic hands swinging like sausage fruit at her side.

The young mother-to-be was lying on a crude bed made of osiola poles tied together with yellow papyrus rope and interwoven with the same stout material. She had just been carried to the Kima Mission on the shoulders of four heathen men whose only clothes consisted of oiled goatskins that hung from one shoulder. Four or five painted warriors were leaping and dancing, jabbing their petal-shaped spears in the air in an attempt to kill the evil spirits that had been refusing the birth of the child.

A larger group of heathen milled in circles nearby, wailing and screaming, their black faces distorted into all sorts of sizes and shapes. The girl's mother, clad only in a dirty loincloth, stood at the end of the bed convulsed with grief. "Oh, Mama, what will I do? What will I do?" she sobbed bitterly. "My only child! My only child!"

As Mother made a hurried examination, an old man with a wrinkled face ran up to the patient and threatened her with his knobkerrie. "Hurry up and deliver that baby or I'll beat you some more, you lazy goat," he shouted, shaking the heavily knobbed club in her bruised and swollen face. "The only trouble with you is that you're a coward. Your husband paid too much for you. You're not even worth a sick rooster. Try harder!"

In one terrible glance, Mother took all of this in. Then she went into action like the heavy tractor Dad had used on his Illinois farm before they had entered the ministry. Her five foot, two-hundred pound frame was stirred to the very depths. "Tsia! [Go!]" she shouted, waving her hands at the crowd.

The people stepped back, but she didn't think they had stepped back far enough. She went after them with blazing eyes and arms akimbo until they were at least fifty feet away. The fact that many of them were armed didn't worry her a bit.

Leading the way, Mother ordered the four heathen men to carry the girl over to the ramshackle, mud-and-wattle hospital at the corner of the mission. This termite-riddled building, with its poorly-thatched, rat-infested roof, was in its last throes. It leaned drunkenly on its cracked sides like an intoxicated colonel. The cow dung-plastered floor had not had a fresh coat of dung for a long time, and so it was full of jiggers. Attractive or not, this building was so crowded that sometimes there were two, and frequently three, patients in each narrow bed.

Actually, the building had been planned for a private dwelling and had been used for that by a missionary family. But when Mother got to the field it was vacant, and so she appropriated it for her medical work. No other building was available.

As the girl was being carried to the hospital, Mother learned that the baby had died in the *etsibadswa* (pelvis) nearly a week before and was still securely lodged there. A witch doctor,

8

with his crude knives, charms, cow dung plaster, and chewed-up grass, had tried to help, but without success. The goat sacrifice had also failed.

There was a tiny kitchen near the hospital. Mother decided this would be her delivery room.

A low window had been built on each side of this stone building, but there was no glass or barrier of any kind at the openings. So when Mother placed the patient on the wobbly kitchen table that Dad had made of packing cases, these windows were jammed with curious and sneering faces.

Mother pumped up a tiny brass primus stove to heat water to sterilize her instruments. This was to be her first *human* maternity case completely on her own. Years before she had performed a Cesarean section on a hog with less than satisfactory results, for the patient and litter had died during the operation.

While she waited for the burner to heat, she prayed for special divine help. Suddenly the door was forced open and a wild-eyed man dressed in a goatskin rushed up to the patient, held her nose shut, and blew into her mouth with such force that his eyes popped and glistened in his black tattooed face like polished cowrie shells.

Horrified, Mother shouted, *"Tsia!* Do you want to kill her?"

"I'm not killing her!" he replied over his shoulder as he fled. "I'm just helping the baby to be born!"

He was a man of courage. The deep scars on his shoulders indicated that he was brave enough to face a leopard. But an indignant white woman with a blue eye and a brown eye was too much for him.

He waited outside just long enough to screw up more courage. Then, when Mother's back was turned, he burst in again and repeated his terrible act. The girl squirmed as he blew, but she wasn't strong enough to get rid of him.

The moment Mother saw him she ordered him out again, but he would simply return a moment later. Mother prayed for patience.

Soon the stove was going and her antiseptic was ready. She

9

started to slip on rubber gloves and get to work when a young man wedged himself in front of her and placed his filthy hands in the solution. Desperate by this time, she sent a Sunday school child to call Dad, who happened to be busy at the workshop.

He came and paced back and forth in front of the door and kept the heathen away while Mother fought for the girl's life. Soon she discovered she needed a tool she didn't have. She explained her need to Dad and he returned to the workshop to see if he could make one.

He found an old gear shift from an ancient Ford truck, heated it on the forge, and hammered it into the proper shape. Then he cooled it in a tub of water and polished the rust and paint off on a grinding stone.

With the help of this tool Mother delivered the baby. Then she made the patient as comfortable as possible. The old heathen mother was overjoyed when she saw that her daughter was going to live. Holding Mother's hand in both of hers, she cried, *"Embuo! Embuo!* [Thank you! Thank you!]"

Mother noticed that the old woman had replaced her loin-cloth with one of the hospital towels. But she decided to close her eyes to the theft. The stars were out and the ou-ja-jah howls of the hyenas in the nearby, granite-covered Bunyore Hills could be heard by the time she was through for the night. But she was happy, supremely happy. A childhood dream of being a missionary had been fulfilled, and she had won her first battle.

As the days went by the slender girl improved. On the seventh day she was able to sit in a chair and listen to the gospel services held in the hospital yard. By the tenth day her appetite had returned, and she was almost well enough to go home.

The mother came each day, after feeding her family at four, and spent the evening with her daughter. The news of the recovery spread through the villages, and even the heathen were saying, *"Nysaye ali omukali!* [God is great!]"* More and more people forsook the witch doctors.

Then tragedy struck.

On the eleventh day the mother pounded on our door, and in a near-hysterical voice, sobbed, "I want Mama! I want Mama!"

When Mother appeared, she grabbed both of her hands and pled, "Come see my daughter *bwangu bwangu* [quickly quickly] for she is dying!"

Without believing what she heard, Mother rushed to the hospital. There she found the girl writhing in agony and spitting up a dark, green liquid. She did what she could to save her, but in two hours the girl was dead.

Mother wept.

That night the cook comforted her. "Don't cry, Missi Ludwig-i," she said, as she struggled with her own tears. "All the people, the Christians and even the heathen, know that God healed her. The witch doctor was jealous. He forced her to swallow poison. He killed her, and everyone knows it."

Soon the funeral horns were blowing and the funeral drums were pounding. Their mournful sound drifted into the mission and cut into Mother's heart like poisoned arrows. The horror of it drove her to her knees. She stayed in that position until courage returned to her heart. Then she got up and made a pot of tea, using the black Simba Chai leaves she had learned to love.

"John," she said, pursing her lips in determination as she looked at Dad, and pounding a tightly clenched fist on the table, "we must do something about this hospital. It isn't right that we have to put up with such a horrible building.

"And we must teach these girls to be better mothers. Ninety percent of their children are dying—dying because of ignorance."

They drank their tea in silence. Then a faraway look came into her eyes. "John," she said grimly while she filled her cup, "we've got to put everything into this work. We've got to work night and day. Kenya has to learn that God is on his throne!" Carried away with her thoughts, she forgot the limit to which one can turn a teapot, and the lid fell onto the cup and broke in two.

Dad started to reprimand her for her habit of breaking teapot lids, when there came a frantic knock at the door. Mother answered it and learned that another difficult maternity case had arrived. Investigation showed that this patient had gone to the witch doctor first and was horribly mutilated. Indeed, the case was so bad the funeral horns had already started to blow.

2

To go to Africa and "proclaim the gospel to the heathen" was the passion of Mother's life. Other things interested her—she was a busy pastor's wife on call twenty-four hours a day—but to be a missionary was her obsession. From the first time she saw a colored person—a slender boy at a fair in McComb, Illinois, when she was eleven—people with dark skins never failed to attract her attention. I knew the story of Robert Moffat and David Livingstone long before I was introduced to the "little red hen."

No author watched the mail closer than Mother. Even though the Missionary Board had turned the Ludwigs down several times, she had absolute faith the Board members would in time change their minds—that a door would open. Once Dad wrote her a long letter, pretending it was from the Board. Then he placed it in a slim, brown envelope—the kind the Missionary Board used—and had me mail it. When it was delivered the next day, Mother's hands trembled as she ripped it open. Dad watched her closely, and I know he felt a little guilty, for Mother's face was radiant as she hungrily devoured the highly enthusiastic letter of acceptance.

Later, when he confessed, Mother's face fell; but she forgave him because of the exultation she had enjoyed for a moment. I was only seven when this took place, but it was such a vivid occasion I remember the details.

Mother had no doubt but that she and Dad would ultimately be accepted as missionaries. She declared that she had received this assurance from the Lord. Indeed, she was so certain that they would serve in Africa, she persuaded Dad to let her go to

New York City where she took an intensified course in obstetrics and tropical medicine at the National Bible Institute.

A year later Father became the fill-in pastor of a church in the Bronx. While there, he enrolled for a six-week program in dentistry in the same school. I remember those days vividly, for when he was learning about molars, I had to open my mouth constantly as he announced the scientific names of my teeth to anyone who was polite enough to listen.

Whenever, after thoughtful prayer and meditation, Mother said a certain thing was going to happen, we all believed it. Her prayers and unwavering faith brought so many things to pass all who knew her marveled. When she prayed for rain we reached for umbrellas. If we told her the request was big, she invariably replied, "And our God is big!"

One evening during the Christmas rush, all we children were with her on the top story of a large department store in Omaha. Our arms loaded with presents, we were eager to go down when the elevator stopped in front of us. It was crowded, but we could have squeezed in quite easily.

Mother started for the door, and then stopped abruptly. "We'll take the next one," she announced firmly, clutching her slender black pocketbook tightly with her right hand.

I pulled at her skirt and coaxed, and my sisters coaxed; but she would not budge. "We'll wait for the next one," she repeated, pursing her lips in a grim determined line—a sure sign that she was certain of her convictions, and that it would be useless to argue or plead.

The next one came, and it was just as crowded as the first. But no sooner had we stepped inside this elevator than the first one fell with a crash. In a moment we were listening to the shrill voices of the passengers frantically shouting for help.

Mother was certain that we had been protected by the hand of the Lord, and who were we to deny it?

For years Mother prayed for Dad's conversion with no apparent results, but she did not give up.

He resisted all the efforts. He was morally clean and had no

13

bad habits. He declared that he was "much better than the hypocrites in the church," and that he didn't see why he should "join up with a crew of lazy professors who let their farms grow up in weeds so they could visit one another and shout about religion."

Dad was practical!

Mother never argued; she prayed. Then one afternoon while he was plowing his Bushnell, Illinois, farm, he saw Mother cross the field and go into a clump of trees. He waited until she was out of sight; then he quietly followed to see what she was going to do.

Hiding behind a tree, he watched as she knelt on the soft grass by a log and began to pray for his conversion. He listened as long as he could stand it; then he quietly returned to his plowing. But he didn't accomplish much. He couldn't erase what his mind had seen and heard.

That evening, after he had milked the cows and fed the hogs, he came into the house and said, "Twyla, I'm going to town. I don't know when I'll be back, but don't wait for me."

He could easily have told her that he was going to a revival meeting, but he was much too proud for that!

He hitched a horse to the shiny, black buggy and drove away. The instant Mother saw the high, narrow wheels disappear through the gate she went into her bedroom, closed the door, got on her knees, and with her face smothered in her hands presented her case to God. She prayed with an insistence that bordered on dictation: "Dear Father, please send John to the revival meeting and please have the Holy Spirit put him under *deep* conviction. Don't let him go over to Uncle Roy's or Father Ludwig's or Father Ogles's. Make him go to the revival meeting!"

She prayed until she knew she had prayed through; then she turned to her mending.

Late that night when he returned, Mother met him at the door with a glowing face. "Well, John, you've got it!" she announced with a triumphant shake of her head.

"How do you know?" he asked, a little surprised.

14

"I know because I prayed through and because I can see the peace in your face," she replied, dabbing at tears of happiness.

Mother had known all along that she and her husband would spend their lives in the Lord's work. She had felt the call ever since her conversion at the age of eleven. But the only one to whom she expressed this feeling was her mother's sister, Aunt Harriet. She had been afraid that if Dad knew it he would be discouraged about becoming a Christian.

Shortly after he put his faith in Christ, Mother became violently ill. She was rushed to the hospital, and there the grim-faced doctors in their starched, white gowns said, "Bright's Disease, double pneumonia, leakage of the heart." It was their considered opinion that she could not possibly live. Brokenhearted, Dad promised God he would do *anything*—even enter the ministry—if only Mother would get well.

Convinced that she would not recover without God's help, Aunt Harriet spoke to her about divine healing. Mother was skeptical. She was certain that healing was for the soul, not the body. Instead of arguing, Aunt Harriet brought her a Bible and a piece of red crayon. "I want you to read the New Testament, Twyla," she said, "and whenever you come to healing, mark the text with crayon."

This Mother did, and to her utter astonishment she found that the Gospels and the Book of Acts were marked from one end to the other.

She put extra heavy markings under such passages as: "And the prayer of faith shall save the sick" (James 5:15). "Again I say unto you, That if two of you shall agree on earth as touching any thing that they shall ask, it shall be done for them of my Father which is in heaven" (Matt. 18:19). "Ask, and it shall be given you; seek, and ye shall find; knock, and it shall be opened unto you" (Matt. 7:7). "Therefore I say unto you, What things soever ye desire, when ye pray, believe that ye receive them, and ye shall have them" (Mark 11:24).

Mother not only marked these passages, but she also read them again and again. They became heavenly bread to her

15

soul. They became a part of the tissue of her life, and she never doubted them for a single moment. Throughout the rest of her career they remained meat and drink, inspiration, and cash in the bank. They became the foundation stones of her house of faith.

She applied these passages to herself and, to the astonishment of everyone, was healed. This experience made a deep impression on her mind, and never could she relate it without deep emotion. It was during this period that she received a definite call from the Lord to go to Africa—a call that had been hinted at in early girlhood.

The promises of God, she was convinced, were completely true. During her later years she testified that God had never let her down on a *single* occasion.

Dad had made a promise. He knew that God had called him to the ministry, but as Mother began to direct his attention to his promise, he hedged. He was already thirty-six and Mother was twenty-seven. He felt they were much too old to start to school again. Moreover, there was a fine "eighty" next to his, and he had decided to buy it.

"With the additional money I will get from this new farm I will be able to support two missionary families," he explained. Instead of replying, Mother prayed.

Then late in the afternoon as he was out plowing, a clear voice seemed to say in a very definite way, "Go look up Isaiah 5:8." He was in the middle of a field when he heard this voice. There was no one in sight. The voice, he decided, was from the Lord. Being a new Christian without the advantage of a Sunday school background, he didn't know where the Book of Isaiah was found. But he was determined to find out, and so he tied his team to the fence and went into the house and got out the Bible.

So unfamiliar was he with the Word, he had to look in the index to locate Isaiah. When he came to the passage he was startled for he read: "Woe unto them that join house to house, that lay field to field. . . ." It seemed the Lord knew all about him!

16

After a long inner struggle he finally agreed that if he could sell the farm he would go to school and prepare for the Christian ministry. However, in order to keep it from selling he set a very high price and did not advertise it!

But the very next day after he had made his decision, a visitor called. "I hear your farm is for sale," he said eagerly at the door.

"Won't you come in?" said Dad, pushing the screen open. Afraid the man wanted to do business, he was coldly polite.

The stranger took a seat by a hanging flower pot and asked the price. Dad named the figure in a tone calculated to make it sound as big as possible.

"That's a lot of money," bargained the visitor.

"It's a good farm," Dad countered, hoping the stranger would lose interest.

The man offered him a price seven hundred dollars lower than he had asked. "No, I want the full amount," replied Dad, his hopes rising.

The stranger gave the flower pot a swing. "All right," he said, pulling out his checkbook. "Here's two thousand dollars earnest money. I'll pay the rest on Monday."

Dad took the check, and with trembling fingers slowly folded it and put it in his blue denims. There were tears in his eyes when the buyer left. He had made a lot of money on the deal, but he loved that farm!

He and Mother stuffed us children into a shiny new Model T sedan and headed off toward Anderson Bible Training School. There were three children. Fern was nine, Rosalyn was five, and I was one. Fortunately, a dedicated lady came to work for them, freeing them for study.

Most of the relatives had been opposed to their entering the ministry. Some even suggested they had lost their minds, or that they were following emotion rather than reason. In order to silence them ever-practical Dad dressed up like a hard-pressed bootlegger. His outfit was complete with a drooping, make-believe cigarette in the corner of his mouth, a dirty cap placed jauntily on his head, and a large clay jug marked conspicuously:

White Mule. He had his photo taken in this costume, and then he changed into the formal clothes of a minister.

He carefully brushed his newly-acquired black suit and, with a Bible in one hand and a brown satchel in the other, had another picture taken. I had managed to slip into the first photograph, but I was too ragged to get into the new one. Next he glued the contrasting photographs back to back and sent them to his complaining relatives, and demanded which career they preferred.

This silenced the opposition as far as the *general* ministry was concerned.

He and Mother were very conscious of their late start in the ministry; and since they could not recall the years they had spent making money, they determined every minute of the future would contain a minimum of sixty seconds of effort put in the Lord's work. Financially independent, they did not have to earn money. But to have a brief vacation or enjoy leisure time was unthinkable.

Within days after their enrollment they were busy in visitation, jail, and hospital work. Father preached his first sermon before a month had passed. Then a J. T. Begley called their attention to a near-empty church building at Ovid, a tiny country town nearby. The congregation had so dwindled that the trustees were being forced to sell the property for a barn. That a church could ever be established in the community was, to thoughtful people, unthinkable. Two large denominations with adequate resources had tried and failed. Mr. Begley, however, believed the right kind of workers could raise up a thriving work. With this thought in mind, he went to several farmer friends and raised enough money to delay the foreclosure.

When Mother and Dad saw the empty white frame building with its tiny steeple and oak pews, they believed God had provided it for them, that it was an open door. After prayer, they agreed to become the pastors. While they were sweeping out the cobwebs and washing the windows, a neighbor came up and asked them what they were doing. When they told him, he replied, "You're crazy. No one can ever gather a congregation here. You're wasting your time."

Mother answered by thrusting a broom into his hands and inviting him to the Sunday services. The next Sunday he was there. Later he became a member.

Before a month had gone by the people in Ovid knew something was happening over at the old community church, and they began to fill its creaky pews. Within a year the attendance shot up to almost one hundred.

Their ministry was practical. They gathered clothes for the poor, got jobs for the unemployed, prayed for the sick, and when a destitute family lost a child they made a wooden coffin for it in addition to taking care of the funeral services. Dad built the coffin out of wood, and Mother lined it with unbleached muslin.

Later they were called to serve a church in Anderson, and then they were sent to Omaha, Nebraska, to open a new work.

There they bought a large brick home for the family and filled it with people in need. No one was ever turned away hungry, and visiting preachers were always extended a helping hand. One time it became so crowded that I had to sleep in the bathtub. When a young pastor from Beatrice stopped with his family and their worn-out car, Dad put them up for the night, told them they could stay as long as they liked, and then, pointing to the bursting and threadbare tires, asked, "How will you ever get to Indiana on that junk? I wouldn't trust them around the block."

"I—I don't know," the man confessed, biting his lip to hide his embarrassment. "But they're all I have. You know our congregation is quite small."

"You'd better pray that God will give you some new tires," advised Dad, making a mental note of their size. "I'd hate to see you stranded." The two of them bowed their heads in solemn prayer and made their request.

Later, when no one was around, Dad called the manager of a nearby garage and ordered five tires, with the understanding that they would be quietly placed on his friend's car at midnight. When the preacher awakened the next morning, he thanked God for answering prayer. Dad believed that God was practical—that he knew people's telephone numbers and addresses. Furthermore, he believed that *he* was one of His servants appointed to help carry out that will, and that this appointment was a *privilege*. In order that he might have more money to help the less fortunate, he insisted on a Spartan economy. Whenever we were on the road, we slept in tents or schoolhouses and ate sack lunches. Father's old suits were made into suits for me, and the scraps were given to the missionaries. "Waste," in our home, was a bad word. He and Mother believed in being practical about everything.

Once when he had me over his knee and was giving me a sound thrashing, I screwed my neck around and pleaded, "You're killing me! You're killing me!"

"No, I'm not," he replied, sitting me in a chair, "and I'll prove it to you." He got out his pulpit Bible and turned to Proverbs 23:13 and solemnly read, "Withhold not correction from the child: for if thou beatest him with the rod, he shall not die." Then, to my added sorrow, he snapped the Bible shut and vigorously continued his correction.

But all Mother could think about was going to Africa. She kept a stream of letters going to the Missionary Board. Finally the Board's resistance wore down, and she and Dad were summoned to appear for conference. "We've agreed for you to go to Africa," said the spokesman, "on condition that you go out and raise enough money to pay your passage, to build a house, and to meet your salary for one year."

The mission to which they were assigned was at Bunyore, near Lake Victoria in the heart of Kenya Colony. This mission, known as Kima, had been founded and financed by a zealous South African lawyer, M. A. Baker. It was a fertile field, and ever since the Board had taken it over in 1922, it had prospered in a most unusual way.

Mother had never raised money before, but with her jaw set firmly, she started out, determined that nothing would stop her.

H. A. Woolman, the pastor in Tulsa, Oklahoma, sent an urgent message not to come. Her immediate reply was, "I'm coming anyway."

He then wired, "Your meeting impossible. We're in a revival."

In reply, she wrote on the telegraph blank in her clear, heavy hand, "Meet me at train depot 10:30 P.M. Saturday."

Woolman met her and diplomatically explained that they were having special meetings, that they were short of funds, and that he could not possibly let her speak.

"That's perfectly all right," she replied graciously. "I need the rest, and if I can't speak, I'll listen to the evangelist."

After going to bed she got her Bible out of the black pocketbook which had started to fatten with letters, addresses, notebooks, and other useful items. Then she opened it to Mark 11:24, and prayed that the Lord would speak to the pastor and allow her to receive an offering. She lay in bed, as was her custom, and prayed until she knew she had prayed through; and then she went to sleep—something the pastor was unable to do.

Woolman rolled and tossed and changed positions in bed. He got up and drank some water; and then he tried to read a book. Finally he said to his wife, "I think the Lord is telling me to allow Twyla Ludwig to speak and receive an offering in our morning service." She agreed and they both fell asleep.

Mother spoke and received one of the largest offerings she had ever received up to that time. Pleased by her spunk, Woolman related the story wherever he went.

Within a few months the entire amount needed was raised, and they started to pack their things. Since my sister Fern was seventeen it was decided she should stay in America and complete her education. This was a hard decision to make, but it was a decision faced by many missionaries in those days.

Bidding the relatives farewell was especially hard. Africa was so far away, and they were getting older. Grandfather Ludwig had become reconciled to their entering the ministry; but seeing them become missionaries—especially to Africa—was almost more than he could endure.

"John, where did you ever get such an idea?" he asked one day, his voice tight with emotion.

"Do you remember the book salesman who called on us in Kansas when I was a boy?" asked Dad gently.

Yes, Grandfather remembered him. He still chuckled at the hard time the Easterner had had scraping gumbo mud off his slick, city shoes. And he also winced as he remembered the difficulty he had had in raising five dollars to pay for the thick maroon copy of Stanley's *Search for Livingstone*. Indeed, he had been forced to pay him in nickles and dimes.

Thinking about it, Grandfather also remembered how Dad used to get out the book, long before he could read, and spend hours looking at the pen drawings of long columns of slaves, with sticks about their necks, who were being driven to the seaports from which they would be shipped to the slave markets of the world.

"That's how I first got interested in Africa," Dad explained. "That book prepared me for the divine call."

"But what are you going to do about the education of your children?" asked Grandfather, placing his hand on my head.

"That's one of the sacrifices that has to be made," said Mother, joining the conversation. "But they'll get to see a lot of things American children never get to see, and I think these experiences will more than make up for what they will lose by not attending the public schools."

The first day at sea was one of my happiest new experiences. Everything was exciting and delightful, especially the dinner table. The bill of fare listed all kinds of foods I had never tasted. And since Dad had informed us that it was all paid for and that we could order anything we liked, I had a wonderful time sending the waiter scurrying after new and exotic dishes. I tasted everything. Then I saw a printed notice at the top of the menu that had, until that moment, miraculously escaped my eye. The notice, printed in big, black letters, read: FRUIT IN SEASON. This was something new and sounded good.

I motioned the waiter over. "Please bring me some 'fruit in season,'" I ordered.

The waiter gulped, choking back a grin. Mother lifted her hands and roared. Rosalyn was mortified. But after Mother had gained control of herself, she said, "That's all right, Charles. This is part of your education!"

Following a week in London we crossed France by rail and then sailed from Marseilles for Mombasa, the gateway to our assignment in Kenya, on the French boat, the *Explorator Grandiddier*.

During our stop at Aden the natives swarmed aboard with all kinds of money-making schemes. Some were selling a jello-like candy known as Turkish Delight. Others would dive overboard for coins the passengers tossed into the water. Leaping from the rail of the ship in graceful dives, they would disappear in the ocean to come up a moment later with a coin glistening between their white teeth. One chocolate-brown fellow, clad in a dirty loincloth, approached us and offered to sing "It's a Long Way to Tipperary" for two francs. After he was paid, he snapped his feet together and said, "What language do you want me to sing it in? I can sing it in French, Russian, Chinese, German, Spanish, Portuguese, Japanese, Hindustani, Kiswahili or English."

We chose English, and he sang it for us twice in his high squeaky voice, rolling his soft, brown eyes and nodding his head in rhythm to the music. Dad said the performance was worth more than two francs and popped another franc into his open, expecting hand.

Along with the various hawkers, money changers, and divers, was a magician. He was a tall Arab with wide sleeves reaching to his slender wrists. His beard was long and white and tapered to a fine point. His specialty was pulling chickens in two. He would wait until a large crowd had gathered; then he would take a chicken in his left hand and while he said, "Gully, gully, gully," pull its head off with his right hand and thus produce two chickens.

Fascinated, I watched him again and again. Sometimes he

reversed the trick. With a chicken in each hand, he would bang them together and make one chicken out of two. The puzzling thing to me was that none of the chickens complained and that the new chicken wasn't any larger than the separate two!

Dad motioned for us to go. "The man's a fake," he whispered. "Let's go to bed."

The Arab turned on him angrily, his black eyes snapping in his sallow face. "Before you go to bed you had better return the chicken you stole," he said caustically.

"I don't have any of your chickens," replied Dad, with genuine disgust.

"Oh, yes you do," said the Arab, taking a step forward. "Look in your inside coat pocket."

Dad put his hand in his coat, and much to his chagrin a peeping chick hopped out. How it got there no one but the Arab knew!

3

On October 31, 1927, the *Explorator Grandiddier* steamed into the channel that led to Kilindini Harbor and the ancient and colorful island-city of Mombasa. Long lines of weather-beaten baobab trees, with their curiously bulging trunks and short, leafless branches stood on the right—grim reminders that although Africa is a land of opportunity; it is also a land of death and sorrow. David Livingstone buried his beloved wife, Mary, at Shupanga under a baobab tree sixty feet in circumference. And behind these trees, jammed full of cream of tartar, were great organized battalions of slender coconut trees, rising to a height of fifty and sixty feet in a humid, cloudless, tropical sky.

Mombasa, one of the most delightful cities in the world, has a sordid history that dates almost to the days of Abraham. Sections of the coastal area were known and developed by the Assyrians as long ago as 2750 B.C. The Assyrians were followed by Egyptians, Phoenicians, Jews, Chinese, Persians, Turks, and Greeks.

The Arabs and the Portuguese also had a strong hand in shaping the country, especially Mombasa. The Turks tossed out the Portuguese in 1585 after they had been ruling for nearly a century. But four years later they returned with reinforcements from Goa, recaptured the island and started to build their famous monument, Fort Jesus. This yellowing masonary fort is still standing and serves as a museum.

Our first view of Kenya made a firm impression on Mother. She wrote:

"As I looked over the motley crowd that surrounded us, there was a chilly, reluctant feeling at leaving the old ship. My husband seemed to shrink. I trembled underneath the awful responsibility. . . . I was so weak I could barely walk. There they were: black people from many African tribes; Arabs from Arabia, Chinese from China, Goans from Goa on the west coast of India, white people from Australia, South Africa, England, America, Europe. . . . They were speaking many languages unknown to us, and these were they to whom we had been sent.

"The Government officials on the shore were speaking Kiswahili to the native porters, trying to get them to hurry in taking the baggage into the Customs House. Each passenger seemed to be trying his best to be first down the gangplank. At last our turn came. We were on African soil!"

On that first day Rosalyn and I perched ourselves atop a huge pile of dull-white elephant tusks in the large, corrugated iron warehouse where the folks were struggling through customs. From this vantage point, our dazzling-white, inch-thick helmets clamped firmly on our heads (Mother would have gotten thicker ones had they been available) and long strips of hideous red flannel pinned on our backs to protect our spines from the tropical sun, we had a fine view of what went on in this Babylon-near-the-Equator.

Swahili women, their short kinky hair parted into many sections, and long veils drawn up to the bridges of their flat, black noses, carried luggage out through the side doors of the warehouse. Indian peddlers haggled over their wares just outside

25

the building; and Arab traders, dressed in white and yellow gowns that reached to the cement floor, came in for their shipments.

That same afternoon, after all the customs had been paid, Dad pulled out our second-class train tickets and hailed a taxi. The little wood-burning train was almost ready to leave when we arrived. He took a quick glance at the engine and sniffed, "In comparison to our locomotives in America this thing looks like a second-rate coffeepot!" Embarrassed, Mother looked cautiously around to see if anyone had overheard. Then she scolded, "John, you shouldn't say such things!"

As we took our seats, Dad replied, "Twyla, I'll quit making fun of their trains if you'll reduce your pocketbook to a decent size. Everyone will begin to think you're a Yankee carpetbagger!"

Mother ignored the remark, placed the pocketbook under the seat, locked the door, and started looking for vermin. She scanned the seams of the lower seats which were to be our beds. Standing on a suitcase, she examined the upper berths with a flashlight. Then she investigated the cracks by the sliding door and the dull-brown framework around the ceiling and lamps. After she had searched every possible nook and corner, she started all over again. Finally, she gave up with the revealing announcement, "I just can't stand bugs!"

The train was now gaining altitude, and as we stared out the windows we found the palm trees, so tall on the coast, were beginning to shorten and thin out. But now the game was increasing. We could see dozens of long-necked giraffe, bare-legged ostriches, herds of zebra, Thompson's gazelles, hartebeests, eland, and many other animals whose names we did not know. Mother encouraged us to watch them—this was to be part of our education.

At dusk, while we were eating the lunches which she had prepared at Mombasa, Mother gave us a lecture on malaria, grimly bearing down with special emphasis on how it is spread by the anopheles mosquito. The point of the lecture was that we must not—definitely must not—sleep with our flesh touching

26

the mesh, for if we did the mosquitoes would stick their bills through and give us the dread disease.

She had just finished in the most solemn tones when a native attendant came in to spray the room with flit, a liquid designed to kill mosquitoes. With vigorous thrusts he sprayed under the seats, over the berths, and into every crevice he could find. Thinking he was through, he started to leave, but Mother wasn't satisfied.

"Now, I want you to spray the children," she said in an even firm voice, as she held the necks of our clothes open.

We didn't want to be sprayed, but Mother had issued an ultimatum, and orders were orders. When we complained she said, "Now, now, now. There's no use in getting malaria even before we get to the mission."

As the train paused at the little station of Tsavo to let off and pick up passengers, Dad reminded us how the man-eating lions had almost put a stop to the Kenya Uganda Railway by eating one hundred and thirty Indian coolies at this place. It all happened as the rails were being laid. The noise of the workmen driving the heavy spikes and putting up the long, steel, American-built bridges frightened the game away. The lions, having nothing to eat, and preferring saltier human beings anyway, proceeded to devour the workmen. At first they were very cautious, only attacking those who had wandered off alone. But as their appetite for men increased, they became more and more brazen.

It was a common thing for a lion to take a man and devour him within a few feet of the camp. Sometimes the man-eaters even took men from moving trains. They would jump into a boxcar, select a victim, and jump out again.

The monsters were quick to develop techniques to get juicy meals with minimum trouble. The terrified coolies began to climb trees to spend the night. Unfortunately, the trees weren't big enough to hold all the men who wanted to sleep in them. The lions, sensing this, would come up to the boma and let out a deep growl. This would send even more men scampering up the trees, and would force the one already perched in a com-

27

fortable crotch to crawl out on a limb to make room for his brother. The lions would then go around the sagging branches of the tree and select the fattest coolie they could find. It was like picking oranges.

This reign of terror continued until Colonel J. H. Patterson, after many tries, killed the brutes and sent their hides to the Field Museum in Chicago where they were stuffed and are now on display.

As we rumbled along in comparative comfort at fifteen and twenty miles an hour and watched the engine belch out great quantities of sparks as it rounded curve after curve, it was hard to believe that we were following the approximate course of the old slave trails. It was even more difficult to believe that there were older people on this same train who had seen those endless columns of slaves, forked sticks around their necks and armed Arabs behind them, treading their painful way to the coast where they were sold to the highest bidder. And yet this was so. Many of the things Dad had seen in the maroon-colored book as a child had taken place on the route we were following.

At one of the stations, I think it was Makindu, a settler's wife got on board and came to our compartment where she declared she had a reservation. This meant that there were five of us and only four berths. But Dad relieved the situation by moving into the guard's van (caboose) and spending the night on a three-legged stool.

Our new companion turned out to be a heavily rouged, hatchet-faced woman with very decided opinions, especially about missionaries and about me—a male—sleeping in the same compartment. She said in her coarse, throaty voice, "It's simply shocking!" Mother defended me, pointing out that I was only nine years of age and sound asleep.

Next she turned her wrath on the missionaries. She said that they spoiled the natives by paying high wages and teaching them to read and write. "If the Government would let the Masai spear the Kukes [Kikuyu], and the missionaries would quit building hospitals and let the niggers die, this could become a decent country. But if we keep going like we are: protecting the Kukes and keeping their brats alive, the colony will get so full of them they'll push the settlers out. . . .

"The year Nairobi was started there weren't any natives for miles around, but look at it now. They're breeding like flies. . . ."

When Mother asked if it wasn't true that the missionaries had pioneered the country, she kept still. But her silence was only for a moment, for presently she started to complain about American slowness in entering the war. "Of course, we would have won anyway," she concluded.

At Nairobi, the capital—a modern city with streetcars, fleets of rickshaws, fine municipal buildings, and an organized crew of men who donned masks and hauled away the sewage each morning before the people got up—we were met by Henry Kramer, the man in charge at the mission. He was short and stout, with a precise, distinguished air about him. He had been converted in San Francisco under the preaching of Dwight L. Moody and was responsible for turning the mission over to its present board in 1922. He had come to take us the rest of the way in his black Dodge touring car.

It took a full day of driving to cover the narrow, treacherous road from Nairobi to Nakuru, a railway town between the capital and Kisumu. On the way Mother's attention was called to a Kikuyu woman. The woman was bent nearly double beneath the load of firewood on her back. It was held in place by a thick leather strap that went around her forehead. There was no danger that the strap would slip off, for it had caused an indentation. Like other Kikuyu women, she had carried unbelievable loads in this manner since she was six years of age.

There were bright-colored coils of beads in the wide holes in the lobes of her ears, and coils of dull copper wire around her arms, forearms, and ankles. The wire was so tight her flesh bulged out like inflated bicycle tubes. A long milk-gourd and a dark brown sisal-string basket dangled from the top of the wood. A naked boy and girl clung to each hand and crouched close to her soft leather skirts as they watched us distrustfully with large almond eyes.

29

Great drops of sweat poured from the woman's closely-shaved head and streamed down her oil-drenched body. The swollen tattoo marks on her stomach indicated that she was expecting a new baby at any time. This may have caused the look of utter exhaustion that masked her round, pretty face.

The tall, well-fed husband, a red blanket tied at his left shoulder, had nothing to carry but a sword-shaped Masai spear.

Mother gasped at the sight. "Why doesn't he help her?" she demanded, her brown eye and blue eye ablaze.

"That's the custom," replied Mr. Kramer gently. "The husband carries just the spear so that he will be free to defend her if she's attacked."

Later, when she learned about female circumcision—clitoridectomy among the Kikuyu and much more savage variations among other tribes such as the Kipsigis—her determination to help native women gained a new depth and a new fury. In later years when she was faced with difficult deliveries caused by the scar tissue formed because of the Kipsigis' version of female circumcision—she made new vows to help the women of Kenya. Mother could never be objective about cruelty to native women. She always felt herself involved. Their tears were her tears; their pain was her pain.

We spent the night in a tiny hotel on the outskirts of Nakuru. The hotel, built of white-painted cedar slab, had less than a dozen rooms and was surrounded with a large, screened-in veranda. Our meals were served by barefoot native waiters dressed in white starched gowns that reached to their ankles. Wearing wide, scarlet sashes around their slim waists and trim, white skullcaps on their shaved heads, they served steaming plates of food with the graceful dignity associated with the world's best hotels. The enormous holes in their ears, the tattoo marks on their black faces, and their sharpened or missing lower front teeth were the only things about them that reminded one that they slept in small, mud-and-wattle thatched huts with cow dung floors and with cattle and goats crowded in the back. It was hard to believe that the slender waiter who poured the coffee with such dexterity subsisted on a diet of blood and milk and that he rinsed the gourds from which he drank his meals with cow urine.

They knew how to fold the heavily starched and spotlessly white serviettes with a deft twist of their slender fingers. They also knew how to toss a native spear or shoot a poisoned arrow.

Suddenly Mr. Kramer reached for the tall amber quinine bottle that stood in its customary place next to the sugar bowl. "I thought I was going to have an attack of malaria," he explained. He placed two five-grain tablets on top of each other between his teeth and washed them down with a swallow of water. "A change of climate always brings it on," he said as a shudder from the taste of the bitter drug crossed his face. "You can generally tell when it's coming because you feel extra strong, and you just can't stop talking. Then you get the chills. The best thing to do is to take five grains every day. But the trouble is the stuff makes my ears ring. Quinine will cure malaria, but you must be careful not to take too much. If you do you may get blackwater fever, and that can kill you in just a few hours."

Mother smiled grimly at the mention of blackwater fever. She knew it was caused by the sudden rupture of millions of red corpuscles which proceed to clog the capillaries of the kidneys. Dr. Stirrett's handbook on tropical diseases had been very explicit. At the first sign of the disease—dark urine—the head of the mission was to "pray to God and send for the nearest doctor."

The quinine, as usual, did its work, and we were on our way to Kisumu the next day. Kisumu, twenty-one miles from Kima, is located on Lake Victoria, the second largest lake in the world. Filled with fish, crocodiles, hippoes, and floating islands, it covers an area a little larger than the state of West Virginia. It was to be our shopping center, for it was the nearest town with a post office, banks, and a telegraph office.

As we drove up the hill toward the bazaar from the freight depot by the lake where we had gone to see if our baggage had arrived, we passed a dozen two-wheeled oxcarts crammed with freight. The spotted oxen, their necks under heavy wooden

31

yokes which pressed against the humps on their backs, strained at their loads, but were unable to pull the carts over the steeper places. A dozen or so workmen dressed in dirty loincloths followed each cart, pushing from behind and pulling up on the spokes.

Streams of sweat pouring off their naked torsos, the workmen chanted native songs while they pushed the carts. Whenever they got stuck because of the steepness of the incline, they would pause for breath while the leader shouted in a singsong voice, "*Elombe, elombe, elombe* [Fix it, fix it, fix it]." On the third *elombe*, which was much louder than the others, they would all shout together, "*Ngufu souwa souwa* [With strength together]." They would let their voices rise on the last syllable and then trail off like a siren. Then they would push together with every ounce of strength they possessed.

The bazaar was made up almost entirely of Indian *dukahs* (small stores) constructed of heavy, zinc-plated corrugated iron with shutters propped up on crude, wooden poles. The storekeepers, most of them hollow-cheeked Hindus with thin black moustaches, were dressed in cotton shirts with unusually long tails extending over their cleverly draped *dhotis* which dropped a few inches below their knees.

They sat on their crude sprawling counters made of pine or cedar with their wares before them in open compartments. Sometimes their bare feet narrowly missed dipping into the sugar, tea, or other staples. Long strings of red peppers hung from the ceiling, and the wobbly shelves on the sides were crammed with bolts of cloth, yard-long bars of blue-mottled soap, spools of thread, and such items as one would find in a tiny American five-and-ten.

Mr. Kramer invited us into a favorite *dukah* owned by Mohammed and his brother, Ali, and asked us to order soft drinks. "I have rose, gingerale, lemon, and lime," said the plump Mohammed with a grand wave of his hand. We ordered rose because, I suppose, it was something new and sounded terribly exotic.

Mohammed waddled over to the shelf where the soda and

32

glasses were kept. He wiped the glasses carefully, polished them with his shirttail and placed them before us as if we were royalty. When he opened the bottles with his pocketknife opener, the soda foamed higher than I had ever seen it foam before. To keep it from overflowing the glasses, he thrust the neck with its thick crust of ancient dirt right into the bottom of the glass. Mother lifted her hands in horror, but the Indian merely smiled, revealing two rows of beetle-nut-stained teeth, and kept on pouring.

While we were drinking the sickly-sweet liquid, a native came in and ordered five pounds of sugar. Ali put a five-pound weight on one side of his old-fashioned scales, lifted them high into the sunlight, and scooped grayish-looking, coarsely ground sugar into the pan on the other side. Then he fashioned a cone from a Bombay newspaper and poured the sugar into it. Next he wrapped the cone with five or six yards of cheap cotton string to keep it from bursting. The native paid him, and asked for *baksheesh*.

In response, Ali tore off a piece of newspaper, put a table-spoon of Simba Chai in it, and handed it to him. This system of *baksheesh*, I soon learned, was always used by the natives.

I decided right then that I would use the *baksheesh* system myself. And my chance to try it came much sooner than I thought it would. As we walked through the bazaar a tall, heavyset Indian with a bulging blind eye and a heavily pocked face kept following us around and staring at the back of my neck. When Dad couldn't stand it any more, he asked him what he wanted.

The Indian pulled a pair of slender scissors from his coat pocket, took a couple of snips in the air, and said, "Haircut, haircut, you wanna haircut?"

Father thought I needed one, and so the man seated me in a store—one of many he used—put a striped cloth around my shoulders, and cut my hair. When he was finished Dad gave him a shilling which was the usual price, and I cleared my throat and asked for *baksheesh*. He responded by pouring some hair oil onto my hair, rubbing it in, and plastering it down.

This barber, like all the other barbers in Kisumu, had a regular route of customers whom he shaved in their stores while business went on as usual. He never shaved the back of my neck. But he was a good barber. He always gave me *baksheesh!*

4

From Kisumu we followed the narrow dirt road that wound around an arm of the lake by Old Kisumu—a line of ancient *dukahs* in the process of being dismantled—and then up over an escarpment through the boulder-strewn Bunyore Hills to the mission. As we bumped along, Mr. Kramer explained how fortunate we were in having a road of any kind.

The first missionaries had had to cover this distance on foot. This had been extremely difficult, for it had been almost impossible to get local porters. Indeed, when Robert Wilson had come and opened the work in 1904, he had had to hire Buganda to carry his loads. The Obunyore wouldn't go to Kisumu for fear of being speared by the Luo, and the Luo wouldn't go to the mission for fear of being speared by the Obunyore.

As we climbed toward the escarpment, we passed many Jaluo, members of the Luo tribe, the second-largest tribe in Kenya and the only major tribe that doesn't practice either male or female circumcision.* The women were completely naked except for a postcard-size black skirt made of beads and sisal fiber. Some of them, in addition to the skirt, wore a thick black tail resembling a fly whisk. The tails indicated that they were married. Almost all of them, especially the older women, smoked foot-long pipes made of clay with straight aluminum stems. The bowls, covered with various geometric designs, were filled with home-grown, pitchlike tobacco.

Elephantiasis had made terrible inroads in this lake area, and we passed many with such enormous legs that their energy was drained just to lift those legs off the ground. Sometimes enlarged from the knee down, they were frequently checkered

---

*This may be a political liability to politicians of this tribe.

34

and were from eight to ten inches in diameter. Watching them laboriously shifting down the road was heartbreaking.

We drove by a small bevy of giggling young girls smoking King Stork cigarettes, the lighted end inside their mouths. This was in direct contrast to the Arabs who, in order to avoid touching tobacco with their lips, place the cigarette between their little and fourth fingers and suck loudly on their doubled fists.

We also passed groups of women with wide baskets of *omabambale* (dried fish) on their heads. These fish, the size of a man's hand, had been split down the center, cleaned, spread open like oyster shells, and dried in the sun. The women, we learned, were traders and were taking their horrible-smelling wares to Luanda and Yala, native markets near the mission.

As we chugged along the eucalyptus tree-lined road that led through Maseno, a large mission sponsored by the Church of England for the Luo, Mr. Kramer informed us that Kima was just three miles away and that we should hold tightly to our seats, for presently we would strike the Equator and the car would jump. We did as we were told and the car bounced high in the air just as he had said. After the bump, I learned that he had hit an enormous antbear hole dug by an antbear in search of a supper the night before. This was one of his many delightful jokes.

When we were just a few hundred yards from Kima, Mr. Kramer said, "There will probably be a few natives out to greet you. The proper salutation is *mirembe*. The word means 'peace.'"

We rounded the last corner, and beginning at Sugar Loaf—a huge rock that stands some seventy feet high and looks very much like a single buck tooth in an old man's lower jaw—there was a long line of Obunyore, thousands of them. The women, clad in white cotton dresses edged in red, and the men, in fresh khaki, were all smiles as we stepped out.

In an instant they were around us, shaking our hands and expressing goodwill. Sometimes they used the right hand, but most of them used both hands, gripping ours very softly in theirs as if afraid they would break or come off. But they did

pump them with great vigor, and occasionally touched our el-
bows, a mark of great esteem. We smiled back at them and
repeated their greetings until we were hoarse.

The twenty-two acre Kima Mission rests in a rock-covered
plateau at an altitude of over five thousand feet in the midst
of the Obunyore tribe who speak Olinyore and who call their
fertile country Bunyore. The site was acquired by Robert Wilson from Chief Otieno in 1904. It was given Mrs. Wilson's nickname, Kima, in honor of her sacrificial labors.

The mission was well kept. There were long lines of eucalyptus trees on either side of its main streets, lovely flowering
poinsettias, full-grown golden and silver wattles, orange, lemon,
lime, and papaya trees, huge yellow and white rose bushes,
frangipani, carnations, and thick clusters of gladiolas. Mother
was delighted.

The main mission house, built of plastered, sun-dried brick
and surrounded with a wide veranda, had a square water tank
at one end into which the rain water poured from the red,
corrugated roof. A thick Bougainvillaea vine with flaming
flowers and purple leaves surrounded the tank and made a
colorful wall along the brown macadam path that led from the
house to the church. A lime tree, covered with fruit, stood con-
veniently just off the north side of the veranda.

Robert Wilson had erected this building a year after his
arrival. He had made the bricks himself. They had not been
burned because he could not procure the necessary firewood.
Much of the lumber had been carried from Kisumu on the heads
of porters, but there were some things which could not be
purchased in the Colony and these were ordered from South
Africa and Sweden. Several years after we had been living in
this house, Dad put a level on top of the doorframe and
measured the side with a plumb bob. It was perfectly square.
Mr. Wilson was a man of many trades and had done his job
well.

But we didn't have time to inspect the mission just then,
for Mrs. Kramer had prepared a sumptuous meal for us. It

was getting dark. Soon our feet were under the long table, the kerosene lamp was turned up, and the conversation began. And what conversation.

Mother and Dad had questions they had wanted answered for years, and now they wanted them all answered at once. And the Kramers were anxious to know the latest news from America. Mrs. Kramer, a brilliant language expert, was then busily engaged in translating the New Testament into Olinyore. This language is filled with the gutteral *kh;* but the sound of the letter x is never used. She wanted to know what Mother thought of substituting the letter *x* for the letters *kh*.

Henry and Gertrude Kramer had four daughters: Mary, a little older than Rosalyn; Gladys, about my age; Romona, who was just learning to talk; and a new baby, Henrietta. Soon the conversation turned to African women, and Mother's interest became even more intense.

Mrs. Kramer explained that there had been sewing classes for the girls. This I knew, for I remembered seeing piles of oblong, brick-sized patches being prepared to send to Africa. By cutting their scraps into this shape, the missionary societies were able to send away more of their scrap material; and the native women got a lot of practice in sewing by piecing these patches together. Besides this, they adored dresses made of countless bright colors. The sewing classes were just getting beyond this stage when we arrived. But I saw many women wearing dresses made of patches. They looked like animated comforters.

Mrs. Kramer also mentioned that many girls attended day classes at the mission and in the village schools. And, in addition to this, there was a girls' dormitory on the mission where the Christian girls could live and thus escape the "pull" of heathenism. But other than these things, very little had been done.

The lack of progress in this field was natural. In heathen days women were kept far behind. This could not be changed overnight. And besides, there was no demand for educated African women. The servants in the homes of the white people throughout the country were all men.

The house we were to occupy temporarily was normally used by Mable Baker, the daughter of the founder, who at this time was on furlough in South Africa. The walls were made of a fragile, bamboo-like reed, tied in place with long strips of papyrus, a tall, triangular-shaped plant that grew in abundance in a swamp near the mission. The floor, like those in the native huts, was made of cow dung mixed with white clay. When I was told this I didn't believe it, for the floors were soft, clean, attractive, and did not have an offensive smell. But when I looked closer and noticed the circular lines made by the fingernails of the girls who had put it down with wide sweeping motions of their arms while they worked on their knees with the mixture before them, I knew it was true.

The kitchen was a separate stone building and was connected to the house by a short, cement walk.

When Dad opened the homemade cedar door, a tribe of green lizards scampered away. I made a dive for one and got hold of its tail, but it quickly disconnected this rather thick appendage and wriggled away through a hole in the wall, its little black eyes grim with fright. There were dozens of hornet's nests hanging from the ceiling which was made of flat papyrus mats, and we had to be careful to keep from being stung.

As we looked over our future home, Dad told us we'd have to be careful and keep the windows and doors closed. "I read of a white man," he said, "who was sitting in his living room with a little dog in his lap. He was just getting up when a leopard jumped through the window, grabbed the dog, and jumped out again." It was a rather gruesome story to precede our first night at the mission, and Mother chided him for it.

When we got to bed Mother saw to it that each one of us was securely covered by a mosquito net. Then she sent Dad into the room with stern instructions to squirt flit into every crevice and corner. This first night etched itself deeply in her mind, as is obvious in the following descriptive paragraphs:

"The scantiness of our equipment was a matter of little concern. We were at last in the 'Promised Land.' The tiny candle we used instead of a lamp or electric lights helped us realize that at last we were on the mission field where conveniences are few.

"We knelt together and prayed to God for a new touch of his protecting and guiding hand. Then we retired for the night, Rosalyn to the little north room and Charles to the west room facing the kitchen. Both of these rooms had dirt floors freshly varnished with cow manure. Mr. Ludwig and I occupied the south room. We were just settled nicely when Rosalyn called out, 'Mother, what's that?' I got up and went into her room and found that it was only a rat peeping through a crack in the papyrus mat used for the ceiling. I tried to comfort her the best I could, and then I knelt by her bed and prayed to God for her protection.

"Then I went back to my own bed. Soon the voice of Charles came to my ears, 'Mother, come!' I got up and went to him. It must have been a hyena that frightened him. I got into bed with him for a while, trying to quiet his nerves; then I prayed for him and returned to my own bed, for the bed he was in was very narrow. That was a memorable night. Strange noises seemed to come from all directions; every little while an owl sent forth its cry, adding to the loneliness of the situation; a woman's voice crying with a sad plaintive sound mingled with words in the native language we couldn't understand; the scream of the hyena as it followed the scent of the dead body with its 'ou-ja-jah,' following the death announcement of the woman, seemed the natural sequence; the funeral drum was heard regularly, followed by the awful thud, thud, of the deadening drum of death.

"I made several trips back and forth to the children's beds; then we put their bedding together on the floor, making a pallet, where I spent the rest of the night with Rosalyn on one arm and Charles on the other. When the morning dawned, a native cook by the name of Zakiah [native pronunciation of Hezekiah] came and offered to help in the preparation of our food.

"Our stove and cooking utensils had not come, so Mr. Ludwig laid up some brick to serve as a stove. There was no oven; so we ate pancakes instead of bread."

Early the next morning, long before sunrise, a native woman with a desperately ill baby in her arms, knocked at our door. She had brought Gladys along to interpret. "My little girl is almost dead," she said between hysterical sobs, 'and my husband will beat me to death if she dies. All my children have been buried but this one. She is the only one left. I have heard that you have good medicines and that you pray for the sick. Will you help me?"

Mother took the child's temperature and made as thorough an examination as possible with the few instruments she possessed. The child, she decided, was suffering from a case of double pneumonia. There was no hospital, and there was no room for the woman in our house, but there was a little space in the kitchen. She led the woman there, gently bathed the child, rubbed its chest with some medicine she had, and got a flannel shirt for it to wear. Then she laid her hands on its head and asked God to heal it. The child began to mend almost immediately and in a few days was completely well.

Mother and Dad determined not to do any active missionary work until they had spent an entire year in language study. With this in mind, and with the warm recommendation of the Kramers, they employed one of the earliest converts, Mathayo, to teach them. Although unacquainted with even the meaning of grammar, he was well qualified for this task because of his slowness of speech and careful pronunciation.

I knew him well, for I used to play with his two younger sons. Not only had he found Christ during the early ministry of Robert Wilson, but he was also one of the first natives to build a square house—a very daring thing to do in those days, for there was a taboo against it. One of his proudest possessions was an unpainted, wooden coffin which stood on end in a place of honor in the front room. Since few if any of the natives had ever been buried in a coffin, this was an envious display.

But my parents' decision to spend all their time in language study was impossible to follow. As the days went by the crowd of sick people demanding attention increased until every morning several hundred had gathered in front of the house to await help. Most of those who called on Dad wanted their teeth pulled, while those who called on Mother had all sorts of tropical diseases.

I can still see her, dressed in a white uniform with a thick helmet on her head, going from one person to the other inquiring about their needs. Having been there only a few days, her vocabulary was meager. She would go up to a woman sitting on the ground with her legs thrust out straight before her—an almost impossible position for an American to maintain for any length of time—and inquire what was wrong. Unfortunately, the only words she knew that related to sickness were *"Indwasi naho?"* This was bad grammar for "do you have a stomach ache?"

Sometimes in reply the woman, with trusting eyes, would point to her shoulders, indicating the bruise marks she had received from a recent beating by her husband. Or perhaps she would hold a gnarled hand over a gash on her head or a wound on her foot or toe. Rosalyn and I were amused at the position of their stomach aches. But the patients never smiled. Their minds were all concentrated on the cure they hoped the short, stout woman of the white man would bring them.

Most of the people who came, however, had huge ulcers. Heavy sticks held firmly in both hands and used as crutches, they would make their way in, hopping on their good leg with the ulcerated one held up behind them or at an angle at one side. Those who could come in this fashion were fortunate indeed. Many had ulcers on both legs and were thus reduced to crawling, and since some of them came from villages miles away, this was a distinct hardship.

A Bunyore ulcer is something you should never see if you want to remain convinced that medical missions are a waste of money. Caused by an inadequate diet, the ulcer is frequently the size of a man's hand. Sometimes this lake of raw flesh— islands of maggots and pus floating in its center and about the edges—reaches to the bone, into the bone, and across a knee

41

or halfway around an ankle or shin. The native treatment is to cover it with mud, or cow dung; or, sometimes, to have a witch doctor spit chewed-up grass into it and over the surrounding area.

In those days there was no cure for such ulcers. All that could be done was to clean and bandage the wound, and this consumed a terrible amount of bandages—especially for the patient who came in year after year with the same ulcer.

Since Mother could not spend her time wrapping ulcers, she trained natives to do this part of the work. But in the beginning it was hard to get a dresser who was completely satisfactory, for all of them insisted on spitting as they wrapped the wound. "You must not spit when you are wrapping an ulcer," she exclaimed on one occasion.

"But it smells bad," replied the dresser, surprised that anyone would object, "and in Bunyore when something smells bad, it is proper to spit."

One morning when there was an unusually large number of patients, a young man by the name of Jairo came in for treatment. He had a deep ulcer on his shin that was steadily getting worse. Converted at a convention years before, he had become a friend of an earlier missionary, Sam Joiner. This missionary had undertaken to teach him English, a subject for which he had great talent.

Mother felt a new joy as she spoke to him in her own language, and she employed him on the spot to help in the mission work. Later on he became Father's interpreter. Intelligent and devout, he was a great help.

Rosalyn and I were very glad that he came, for we were getting tired of being called from our play to interpret for someone who was positively certain the witch doctor had placed a pair of shoes in his chest. Dolls and spears and bows and arrows were much more interesting than ulcers, bad teeth, and women who had been beaten half to death by angry husbands. One man who had been bitten by a snake made the mistake of going to the witch doctor first. The medicine man put a tourniquet on his arm; he had probably seen a white man do this. But instead of taking it off in a few minutes, he left it on for three days. The man's arm was completely withered; the fingers were like shriveled green beans. One could have cut his hand off and he would not have felt it. Dad rushed him to Maseno where his arm was amputated at the shoulder.

Another patient had tried to commit suicide by cutting his throat with a Bunyore dagger. He had made two long slashes, but both of them had only gone deep enough to expose his windpipe. The brownish, corrugated tube stood out in bold contrast to his unusually black skin.

After the second slash he had decided that he wanted to live and had gone to the witch doctor, who sacrificed a red rooster, said some magic words, and covered the jagged wounds with a fresh layer of cow dung.

Had Mother been there Dad would have turned him over to her, for she had had a year of medical training while he had had none. But since she was unavailable, he took charge. Not knowing where Mother kept her surgical thread and needles, he washed the wound with raw alcohol and sewed it up with a darning needle and white thread. I thought the thread should have been black to match his skin, but Dad disagreed. The man lived.

The next man to be treated had been bitten by a black mamba. His hand was more than double its normal size. Again Dad took charge. He placed a tourniquet on his arm and lanced his hand with a razor blade to let out the poison. Unfortunately, he cut an artery and the blood squirted out in a sudden crimson stream. Seeing the blood, the patient took to his heels and the tourniquet came off as he ran. Dad shouted at him frantically trying to turn him back. But the louder he shouted the faster he ran. Father knew that if he wasn't repaired immediately death would follow. He also knew that if this happened he might be charged with manslaughter, even though he had done his best under the circumstances.

A tall Bunyore youth of fifteen or sixteen who had been standing nearby sensed the situation immediately and started after the fleeing man. Luckily, he caught him and brought him back. Dad had his patient repaired, blew a sigh of relief, and decided to leave such cases to Mother.

The natives continued to come in throngs for prayer and medical aid. After a staff meeting it was decided to use an old mud-and-wattle building on the other side of the mission for a hospital. This building was on the verge of collapse, but Dad had new thatching grass put in the roof where it leaked, had the floor varnished with a fresh coat of dung, filled it with twenty-five or thirty native beds, and dignified it with the name "hospital." This was pronounced "hospital-i" by the natives, for the Obunyore find it almost impossible to end a word with a consonant.

From the opening day the "hospital-i" was crowded with patients. Sometimes there were two and even three in each narrow bed. They would jam themselves in by alternating their heads and feet like sardines. There was no time for language study, and so Mother wrote Olinyore words on scraps of paper and memorized them as she worked.

Hezekiah was a good cook and provided an excellent table. He had learned the trade in Nairobi and was an expert. He knew the food we preferred and worked hard to prepare it. I used to visit with him while he toiled in front of the kitchen table. Dressed in a starched white gown with a matching skullcap on his shaved head, he would tell me about the woman with eighteen children while he sliced the carrots with his favorite knife.

The Obunyore felt that eggs with "a little meat in them" were better than fresh eggs, and to keep from buying such eggs he would *pima* (test) each one in a bowl of water. In order to pass his rather strict requirements it was necessary for the egg to lie completely level on the bottom. A slight tilt was enough to have it rejected.

Since Hezekiah was the cook, and since this was a very honorable position with high social overtones, he insisted that someone else be employed to wait on the table, cut the wood,

44

and keep the fire going. That person just "happened to be available, and so it was that a young Bunyore with the appropriate name of Shadrach—pronounced by the natives *Sadoka* —was hired to keep the fires going.

5

I asked a friend the name of the boy who had caught the snake-bite victim. "Oh, that's Samwelli," he replied, lifting his eyebrows in surprise that I didn't already know. "He's the son of Isaiah and Phoebe, who were among the very first converts."

As I looked at Samwelli with his broad shoulders, wide smile, and clear-cut features, I could see that he had had a very positive Christian background. For, unlike the heathen, he still had his six lower front teeth, there were no tattoo marks on his face or abdomen, and his ears did not have holes in them. Moreover, he had an insatiable desire to learn.

From the very beginning Samwelli and I became warm friends, and almost all that I learned about native customs, I learned from him and his friends.

His parents, and especially his mother, were people of great courage. They defied the witch doctor at a time when his power among the people was absolute, and they defied him with a cool boldness that made the heathen shake their heads.

Americans have an inclination to hold all witchcraft up to ridicule. This is a grave mistake. The witch doctor does have a dreadful, sinister power. Scores of people die every year because of his curses and medicines. Dr. Willis R. Hotchkiss, a distinguished missionary to Kenya for many years, was convinced of this power through bitter experience. In his book, *Then and Now in Kenya Colony*, he wrote: "It will not do to dismiss this witchcraft business with a shrug and say there is nothing to it. There is something to it and that is what makes it a thing to be reckoned with."[*]

———
[*]*Then and Now in Kenya Colony*, by Willis R. Hotchkiss. Copyright Fleming H. Revell. Used by permission.

If you visit any hospital in Kenya, the doctor will tell you of cases where people have died because of witchcraft. Undoubtedly there are scores of scientific explanations, but the fact remains that the people die. No one can deny that. There is too much evidence.

Mother soon learned that the Obunyore are ruled by all kinds of taboos. These strictly enforced restrictions are decided by the witch doctors and generally work to the advantage of the men. For example, there is a taboo against eating chicken. If a woman were to even take a tiny bite—except under unusual circumstances such as having given birth to a son—she would, according to the medicine man, face the possibility of having twins. And having twins would be one of the worst things that could happen. In the old days the twins would have been murdered. Since they believe a man can only father one child at a time, it is evident the other is fathered by an evil spirit. Of course the *real* reason for the taboo, Mother decided, is that there are not many chickens and the men are very fond of them.

Another taboo states that women are not to eat eggs, and another insists that women are not to take their babies with them when they dig their husband's gardens. The reason for this last taboo is that if they take their infants to the gardens they will have a tendency to look after them and neglect their work. All babies are supposed to be left at home in the care of a nurse girl, even though the nurse girl may only be a year or two older than her charge.

A heathen woman would as soon put a razor to her throat as to break a taboo. Mother despised these taboos, and when she thought about them her blood pressure went up.

When Phoebe accepted Jesus Christ she declared that she was not only through with the world—her pipe, beer, and dishonesty —but also with all superstition. She announced that she was no longer afraid of even the most famous and powerful witch doctor. This was an extremely brave stand, for all her relatives had believed in these things for countless generations. She herself had witnessed many a death caused by the curse of the witch doctor. But now her faith in Christ was so great she publicly scorned witchcraft in spite of the unbelievable horror of her friends.

Her stand was known throughout all of Bunyore. It was the chief topic of conversation when the women bathed at the river in the valley south of the mission, or sold their produce in the market at Luanda. It was what the young men discussed as they mudded their faces for a funeral dance or a beer drink. And although the missionaries encouraged her, the heathen shook their heads and predicted bad results. One close relative spoke for the entire heathen community when she said, "Phoebe has lizards in her head. She has even started to eat eggs and chickens. Now she'll have twins!"

On a late afternoon she was confronted by her sisters just as she was returning from the river with a pot of water on her head. "We have come to tell you," said Olioti craftily, "that we don't care because you are a Christian. You made that decision yourself. But this new baby you are going to have belongs to us. We want you to let us make a sacrifice for it so that it will grow up to be a healthy child."

"My faith is in Jesu Christo, and not in witchcraft!" replied Phoebe as politely as she could. "Jesu Christo was the great sacrifice. No more are needed."

"For this we won't help you when your child is born," sneered Olioti angrily. "We'll leave you all by yourself and you may die. But we won't care!" She emphasized her words by spitting on the ground and then stomping in the pool of spittle.

Phoebe's husband who had been a Christian for several years overheard this last remark. "Never mind," he said, rubbing his smooth chin thoughtfully. "I will help you!" This was an amazing thing for a Bunyore to say. To the heathen it was equivalent of saying, "Get a rope. I want to hang myself." Men, even the best men, did not help their wives at such times. It was taboo.

When a Bunyore woman knows that her labor pains have begun, she goes behind her hut, out of sight, and hides in the banana trees like a wounded animal. Then she makes a soft

47

pile of banana leaves to receive the baby and sits over them on a thick stick placed vertically on the ground.

During the agony of labor the mother-in-law often squeezes the struggling woman's nose between her thumb and forefinger and blows into her mouth, hoping her breath will aid in the delivering. And between pains she generally makes use of the time by reminding her daughter-in-law that the new life belongs to her son and that if it dies it will be because of her laziness.

If the child does not breathe when it is born, the old women, who have gathered by this time, fan it with banana leaves. Should this fail, the mother holds the baby's mouth and nose to her mouth and sucks out the mucous that is stopping up the air passages. After its first cry, she ties the umbilical cord with a piece of banana bark, cuts it off with a sharp blade of grass, and motions for one of the old women to bend over and draw on her pipe. While the tobacco glows she presses the end of the cord into the coals and thus cauterizes it.

This accomplished, she asks for a *jembe* (a short-handled, heavy-bladed hoe), struggles to her feet, digs a hole by the side of her hut and buries the placenta. If the husband is around he watches with pride.

The heathen were outraged at Isaiah's suggestion, and predicted that all kinds of misfortune would come to him. But he and his wife merely laughed. They had complete confidence in Jesus Christ. In due time the baby was born and everything went according to schedule. She named the girl Gibisonia.

A few days later the sisters returned. "All of us are glad that the baby is all right," said Olioti smoothly, trying a different approach. "It's a very nice baby and looks just like you. But you had better let us make a sacrifice for it or it won't live."

Phoebe shook her head. "When I became a Christian I gave up all heathen sacrifices."

"If you don't let us make a sacrifice," warned Olioti, "we won't send you a nurse girl to take care of Gibisonia while you work in the garden. And if you don't get a nurse girl, you will have to stay at home. Your husband will then beat you for not digging his property."

"I'm sorry that you refuse to send me a nurse girl," said Phoebe with a smile. "But if you don't send me one, I will take her into the garden and leave her in a basket while I work."

At this the sisters' faces became as black as cooking pots. "You wouldn't dare take your child into the gardens," they gasped, putting their hands over their mouths. "If you do the witch doctor will—"

"My trust is in Jesu Christo," interrupted Phoebe. "He has helped me in other matters. He will help me in this."

She took the child with her to the gardens. As the heathen watched her making her way through the winding paths to her place of work, they scoffed and spat and sneered. But Phoebe ignored them the best she could, and nothing unusual happened.

The sisters, however, would not give up. "You look nice in your new dress," said the youngest of them one afternoon just before the evening meal. "I suppose very soon you will be wearing shoes like the woman of the white man!"

"No, I don't think I will ever wear shoes," replied Phoebe, forcing herself to smile. "But I'll never give up my belief in Jesu Christo. He is my very life."

Gibisonia grew up to be a fine girl, and when she was baptized she changed her name—as was the custom among the Christians—to Neva. Samwelli was the next child.

Huge granite boulders were strewn about the mission just as they were throughout the surrounding villages and on the nearby Bunyore Hills. Many of them were as large or larger than a three-bedroom house. They looked like square and round and oblong loaves of bread waiting to be buttered. These boulders absorb the heat during the day and radiate it at night. In the evening, after a hot day, one can see a thin mist rising from their warm, smooth sides.

At that time Kima had about a dozen buildings. Most of them were built of red burned brick pressed out on the mission press and carried to location on the heads of the women who protected their skulls with a doughnut-shaped *ligari* made of banana leaves. Nearly all these buildings were roofed with native thatching grass, and these remarkably cool roofs were from six to eight inches thick.

The biggest project on the mission was the foundation of the new church building—a huge fortress-like affair designed to seat from two to three thousand. But funds had run out before the walls could be finished, and in most places they were only three or four feet high. During the rainy seasons the rain poured down on these unfinished walls, and each downpour did a certain amount of damage. But there was nothing that could be done about it, for there was no money.

A football field spread out on the east end of the mission just north of the new church foundations, and was in constant use. Football—European soccer—is very popular throughout East Africa. The natives play barefoot and kick the ball with the sides of their feet. They have remarkable control. I have seen a player curve the ball through the goal with a corner shot, a most difficult thing to do. Since football is much less harmless than tossing spears in cattle raids, the government has encouraged it. In my early teens I had an excellent Eleven, Teamu Mambu. I fitted them out with striped T-shirts which I had purchased from an Indian in Kampala. When this team trotted out onto the field, their shirts clinging to their powerfully built arms and chests, they looked like escapees from a Georgia chain gang. But this was the proper uniform and their appearance always brought shouts of admiration from the crowds that stood around the edges of the field.

As the game progressed, I used to run up and down and shout encouragement to the players. I knew all of the special names given to them by their admirers, and these names—descriptive of their special abilities—I shouted at the top of my voice. There was a short player known as Engini Majewa because when he ran his legs went back and forth with the speed of a piston in a one-cylindered engine. Then there was Karadasi Budotindo. He got this name, which referred to paper, because he could leap high in the air like a scrap of paper in a whirlwind. My shouting was always very helpful. This team never lost a game. But on one occasion we just managed to tie, and we only did that because of the special strategy I employed.

Seeing that we were losing by a score of one to nothing, and that we only had a few minutes left, I rounded up all the mission girls I could find and sent them over to the game. My instructions were clear: "Shout, scream, call out favorite names, jump!"

At first the bewildered girls obeyed simply because of my instructions. But within minutes they got into the spirit of the game and began to shout at the top of their voices. The inspiration of their white dresses, shining heads, scrubbed feet, and glistening shins was all that was needed. At the last moment Engini Majewa caught a sizzling ball on his forehead and sent it through the goal. The crowd went wild. Our record wasn't broken.

One afternoon, just after we had arrived at Kima, Samwelli took me down to Palace Rock in the valley on the west side of the mission. Palace Rock—Mr. Kramer gave it this name, I believe—is an amazing natural formation. Three granite boulders, each the size of a modern Greyhound bus, form a tepee-shaped triangle on top of another wide, flat boulder. And, to make the shelter complete, there is a table-sized stone with a reasonably flat top in the center. It is an ideal place to go for picnics and is almost stormproof.

From this vantage point, we had a panoramic view of the country around us. "That long line of trees over there on the northeast," he said, "is the Boma. That is where the government collects taxes.

"Every year on the right date, they bring a lorry full of soldiers, run their *pendera* [flag] to the top of the pole and take the people's money. Each person has to pay fourteen shillings. Twelve shillings are for Bwana D. C. and two shillings are for the chief. The chief eats more shillings than anyone else in Bunyore. Of course if a man has more than one wife, he has to pay another tax on each woman. Our chief, Zakio, has

51

eight or maybe even seven wives and so he has to pay a tax on each one."[*]

Samwelli then pointed to a triangular haze of blue to the north. "That is Mount Elgon. It is one hundred or maybe even ninety miles from here. The elephants live there and so do the Wagishu. They are cannibals. Our other mission is at Ingotse. It is forty miles from here, and you pass it on the way to Mount Elgon. The people there are called the Butsotso. Their language is almost the same as ours. But they have plenty of land. All you have to do to get land for a garden is to tie some grass together along the border you want to reserve, and it is yours for that year.

"I wish we had that much land in Bunyore," he added, pointing to the many clusters of huts that nestled on every hill. "The Baileys and the Murrays are our missionaries at Ingotse."

All at once he brought me back to earth by saying, "The sun is going to bed. This means we'd better go home, for this is the time *Bwana Chui* [leopard] likes to go for a walk, and I don't care to meet him."

"Do the leopards ever kill people?" I asked.

"Oh, yes, they kill lots of them. But leopards don't eat people. They just let them lie around for the hyenas."

6

One afternoon, just after lunch, Samwelli's sister, Neva, knocked at the door and applied for work. "What could you do?" asked Mother, noticing her red-trimmed dress and the white cloth tied around her smoothly shaved head.

"I could sweep and help in the kitchen," she replied, her large brown eyes focused on the ground. This kind of work was needed, and so she was hired at a wage of four shillings (then one American dollar) a month.

Neva learned rapidly and in a matter of days was washing

---

[*]According to one interesting story, some white scoundrel got hold of a British flag, raised it, collected the tax money, and then fled the country.

and drying the dishes, carrying heavy pots of water from the valley, and bringing in the firewood for the stove.

After she had been with us about a month, Neva announced that she just could not do all the work and that a helper was desperately needed. When Mother asked whom she could suggest, she motioned for her friend Haabwe, who was standing nearby, to come over.

Haabwe, perhaps a year older than Neva, had had smallpox; and, in order to enhance her beauty, she had carefully picked her face until it was covered with a mass of pits. Her skin was a shade lighter than Neva's, hinting at a touch of Arab blood. And, unlike Phoebe's children, she had been raised in a heathen home and thus had had her six lower front teeth pried out. Her father had been a halfhearted Christian, had been baptized, and had changed his name to Elijah. But unlike his famous namesake, he had stayed under the juniper tree until he had given up his profession altogether, even though he lived right on the southern border of the mission.

Mother interviewed her carefully, and then engaged her to carry water. She was a hard worker and from morning until night kept busy, going back and forth to the spring with a huge black pot on her head. As she delivered the water, Neva boiled it to make it safe for our use.

There were a great number of wild red berries nestled among the slender eucalyptus trees in the valley by the spring, and Haabwe soon learned that we—especially Mother—were very fond of them. They were about the size of a large thimble, were hollow and had a flat, strawberry taste. Whenever she wanted to please us, she would gather a pan of them and place them on the table.

Father and Mother worked hard at learning the language, and whenever they learned a new word they tried to press it into their minds by using it. Once, late in November, in order to use a new word and to impress on Rosalyn and me the progress he was making, Dad summoned the cook. Then in solemn tones ordered him to get a *likhoondo* and make a pie. Hezekiah tried to hide the smile that tugged at his lips, but he could not;

and Rosalyn and I broke into peals of laughter, for instead of telling the unfortunate man to get a *lihoondo* (pumpkin), he had told him to get a monkey!

Haabwe heard our laughter and was indignant. "You shouldn't laugh at your father," she scolded. "Those two words, *likhoondo* and *lihoondo*, sound almost alike. And they're almost the same in your language, too."

"Oh, no they're not," I argued.

"Yes they are," she contended, her face getting a shade blacker and her lip trembling in anger. "In the words of the white people you call one monkey and the other punkey and I can hardly tell one from the other!"

Rosalyn spent a lot of time teaching the girls English, and they absorbed it like a sponge. As Mother watched their progress she kept saying, "See, these girls are not stupid. They can learn like anyone else, and the sooner we establish a school for them the sooner we'll get a New Africa. 'The hand that rocks the cradle rules the world!' "

As Mother learned more about the inhuman way that the native men treated their wives, she became more and more incensed. I remember sitting with her in the car on a moonlit night near the chief's village and watching a woman get a *jembe* and bury her placenta in front of the hut. As Mother watched the woman sway on her feet as she dug the pit, she bit her lips and her cheeks moistened with tears. She was never able to shrug off wife beating as did others. An African woman to her was not just a woman born in dreadful circumstances, but a human soul for whom Jesus died. And the more she became incensed the more she was determined to do something about it.

On a July evening just a few minutes before the sun would be flaming over the horizon, a heathen man dragged his wife into the mission and knocked at our back door. "I want you to help my wife," he said, pointing to a deep gash in her side.

A quick glance showed that a forked stick had entered her body just below the rib cage and pulled out the tip of her lung. This bit of lung, about the size of a fried egg, had been plastered with cow dung; and crude efforts had been made to push it back in place. The woman was so faint she rocked on her feet as Mother examined her.

"Who did this?" asked Mother, her eyes beginning to blaze.

"Well, I-I beat her because she's lazy," answered the broad-shouldered man, shifting his feet nervously. "As I was beating her she turned and my club broke. It's all her fault."

"But you have no right to beat your wife," interrupted Mother, her voice getting taut in spite of determined efforts to remain calm.

"I paid five cows, four goats, and twenty-four shillings for her," he replied haughtily, "and I can do with her what I please. She is my property! If she hadn't been so lazy I wouldn't have had to beat her. It takes a lot of effort to get five cows, four goats, and twenty-four shillings."

Mother had the woman taken to the hospital, and after she had washed the wound with alcohol, put her to sleep, cut off the protruding piece of lung, sewed up the cut, and put her to bed. Then she sat down with the man and proceeded to tell him what a horrible thing he had done. "And now your wife may die of infection. If she dies you will be a murderer and the Government may hang you!"

The reality of his plight suddenly came to him and he visibly shuddered. A man near his village had been hanged a few months before, and he knew it could happen to him. Mother took advantage of the situation at once.

"Your wife will need some good food in order to gain strength," she said, "and so I want you to go back to your village and get the fattest *inyabuli* [hen] that you have and bring it here and cook it for her."

"But black women don't eat chicken," he replied, a silly grin on his face and his eyes on the ground.

"Others may not eat chicken, but this one will," replied Mother slowly and deliberately, her lips in a fierce, determined line. The unfortunate man returned to the hospital, viewed his wife to make sure she was still alive, and then went after the hen.

An hour later he returned with a live chicken and handed it to Mother by the feet. "Your wife can't eat it alive," she said, shaking her head. "You must go to the valley and get some water and clean it and cook it for her."

"But Mama," he pled, "Obunyore men don't carry water."

"It may be that others don't, but you will," she said, looking him right in the eye. "And you had better hurry because it's getting late."

Reluctantly he got a *debi* and headed for the valley, his feet as heavy as rocks. In time he returned with it half full and showed it to Mother.

"Now, you'll have to get some firewood and cook it," she said.

"But the men in our tribe don't gather firewood," he complained bitterly. "That's a woman's job."

"Maybe other men don't gather firewood," conceded Mother, her lips tighter than ever, "but you will!"

When he hesitated she reminded him that he might be hanged, that the gallows were just as close as his wife's death. And so, in utter desperation, he moved his goatskin from his right shoulder to his left shoulder and started to look for wood. Fortunately, it was nearly dark and no one was able to see his humiliation.

About an hour later he had a fire going and was boiling the chicken. His wife, of course, was too ill to eat any of the actual meat, but Mother had the broth taken to her, and for the first time in her life she tasted chicken.

But this wasn't the end. Mother, as always, felt she must have the last word. She led the husband to a private place and then she said, "Your wife may die after all. God is the only one who can keep her alive, and so let us pray together." The two of them got on their knees—he for the first time in his life—and Mother prayed that the woman might live and that both she and her husband would become Christians. The woman recovered, the family honored Christ, and happiness was restored to the home. Mother considered the episode a personal victory.

Often a man would come in with the report that a leopard was stealing his sheep and demand that Father come with his *bunduki* (gun) and shoot it. Then, of course, there was the usual crowd which came in to have their teeth pulled. Dad became an expert at this. He never used an anesthetic of any kind, but his forceps were so much easier than the witch doctor's knife and rock that he had hundreds of patients.

One of his patients, however, would not leave after his extractions. And since Dad had not yet learned the language, he called Jairo to interpret. Then he discovered that a former missionary had pulled one of his teeth years before and had given him some yellow pills to take.

Knowing that he would not leave until he was given something, Dad went into the house and filled a little amber bottle with a heavy concentration of salt water. Then he pasted an impressive label on the front with the words "Aqua Pura and Sodium Chloride" printed in heavy red letters. As he handed it to the grateful man, he warned him solemnly, "Be certain never to take more than three spoons of it in a single day!" The patient left grinning from ear to ear.

One of the callers at the back door was a little old woman. Her face was as black and as wrinkled as ancient shoe leather, and I am sure there wasn't a tooth in her mouth. Except for a tiny black bead skirt, she was entirely naked. When we opened the door she was sitting on the ground for the simple reason that she was too feeble to stand.

When Mother asked her what she wanted, she replied brokenly between sobs, "Oh, Mama, I have come to you because my old man has beaten me and sent me away, and I have no place to go. My children are all dead and I don't have any friends."

"Where are you from?" asked Mother.

"My hut is in Marigole on the other side of Ebwali," she replied, a look of terror in her dim eyes. "But, please, don't send me home!"

The place she indicated was four miles away, and since she had crawled the entire distance on her hands and knees, it would have been heartless to have sent her back. Although there were no facilities on the mission to take care of people in her condition, there was an old hut near the house where the Kramers lived. Mother decided to send the woman there. She was given a calico dress, and I was assigned the job of taking her food every day.

This little old woman—Omukhasia was her name—was very receptive to the gospel. Haabwe and Neva spent a lot of time with her. And since she was too feeble to care for herself, they washed her and took the jiggers from her hands and feet.

Omukhasia was happy at Kima. She would creep over to the hospital and listen to the gospel as it was presented every morning, and then crawl back to her hut with a new light in her face. She accepted Christ as her Savior the very moment she understood what it was all about. But as she grew stronger spiritually, she became weaker physically. After a month or so she only managed to get to the hospital with the greatest difficulty.

About the time her wounds were healed she crawled over to our back door and asked to see the woman of the white man.

"What do you want?" asked Mother, bending low so that she could hear.

"Oh, please, Mama," she replied, her voice trembling with fear and emotion, "I want to go home because I heard my old man died."

"But he beat you. You wouldn't want to go back where he lived."

"It is true that he beat me, Mama," she replied dropping a tear, "but he was my old man just the same and I loved him."

"But if you go back, there will be no one to take care of you. You said that your children were all dead."

"Mama, I'm not going to live much longer. I want to go back so that I can see his grave and curl up on the floor of our hut and die in the same place where he died."

58

Mother refused to grant the permission, knowing that the trip would shorten if not end her life. I was instructed to keep an eye on her to see that she didn't leave. But one morning when I went to her hut I found that she was gone. I made inquiries and Haabwe told me what had happened the next day. Starting long before sunrise Omukhasia had crawled the entire distance to Marigole. It probably never occurred to her that she might be killed on the way by a leopard or hyena.

When the people found her she was in her husband's hut, and those who knew said that she died in the same spot where her husband died. When they found her, her body was quite cold; but there was just the trace of a smile on her lips.

I remember a morning when a sobbing woman came with a year-old baby in her arms. "My baby is dead! My baby is dead!" she sobbed. "Call Mama at once and have her pray for it!"

Mother felt for the pulse without finding it. Then she listened with her stethoscope for the heartbeat, but if there was one she did not hear it. However, the child was still warm.

She ordered Haabwe to heat some water on the stove, and then she requested the mother—she was a Christian woman—to agree with her in prayer that God would heal the child. When the water was hot she poured it into a shallow basin. Then she submerged the baby—first in hot water and then in cold water—and gave it artificial respiration while she prayed. She kept repeating this process and it seemed to me she was wasting her time.

Suddenly a bubble of mucus formed in the baby's left nostril. It grew larger and larger, glistening in the harsh sunlight. A miracle had been performed! The child remained in the hospital for a few days and then returned with its thankful mother to the village.

Mother's fame spread throughout the villages, and she found herself working night and day, delivering babies, praying for the sick, giving simple medicines, and dressing ulcers. Illnesses that could not be helped stirred her sympathies, but when she came face to face with disease and death that was caused by cruelty, carelessness, or even ignorance, her brown eye and blue eye blazed with determined wrath.

Seldom did a week pass without a child being brought in that had crawled into the fire smoldering in the center of the hut. Frequently these babies were so severely burned that nothing could be done but to make them as comfortable as possible until death mercifully took them. And occasionally a frantic mother would race into the hospital with a little fragment of humanity that had been stepped on by a careless ox stalled in their hut.

In spite of the inadequate medicines, leaky roofs, spittle-laden cow-dung floors, and the lack of trained personnel, many hundreds of people were cured every year. Even so, the witch doctor continued his horrible trade, and Mother saw the results of his mutilations every week. She knew that the only remedy was to train the wives, and show them a better way. Denouncing the witch doctor would only help his cause.

Samwelli and I were sitting in Palace Rock eating sugarcane when the conversation turned to the hospital and the white man's medicines. "The white people have wonderful *dowa* [medicine]," he said, as he cut off a two-foot length of sugarcane with his grass knife. "But the best of your medicines are not half as good as what the witch doctors used to have a long time ago."

He struck the end of his sugarcane on the rock until it was frayed, and then he tore off the tough bamboo-like bark with his strong white teeth, exposing the sugar-laden pulp within. "Many years ago the Obunyore witch doctors had marvelous medicines," he explained while he chewed the pulp and swallowed the juice. "Now look at Ebitanyi. If he had been living then, instead of cutting off his leg as you white people did, the witch doctor would have fixed it."

I knew Ebitanyi. I remembered how he had hobbled into the mission with a huge ulcer on his knee, and how this leg was withered until it was only two-thirds the size of the other one. But I had just recovered from an attack of malaria and wasn't in the mood to argue, and so I said, "I don't want to argue, Samwelli, but I don't see how that could be possible."

"Listen, and I'll prove the superiority of the witch doctor quicker than a woman can spit when she smells something bad," he said with a boastful tilt of his chin. "I had a friend by the name of Omucara. He wanted to get married, and so he sent a friend to another village to look for a wife for him. This friend found a girl who lived at Luanda. She was a wonderful girl, plump and strong. She could carry more water than anyone else in the village, and she could dig all day long in the gardens without getting tired. More than this, her skin was light brown and she had a fine set of tattoo marks on her face and stomach.

"But her father knew she was a good possession and demanded a large dowry. Omucara only had three cows, and they were so thin one could almost see the grass in their stomachs. When he offered the cows to the girl's father, he refused him. Omucara then tried to get her on the installment plan. But the old man still refused. He said that one cow in the hut was worth more than three cows in the head—that he would rather see one cow than hear about three.

"Omucara tried to forget the girl, but she was so plump and strong he could not. Finally, he decided to go to Nairobi and get a job and work until he had eaten enough shillings to buy the cows to pay for her.

"He got a job with a white man, and because he worked hard he ate sixteen shillings a month. After a while he had enough shillings to buy the necessary cows and goats. But when he went to his *bwana* and told him that he wanted to quit so that he could go home and buy a wife, the white man refused. And, as you know, if you get a job in Nairobi, or Kitali, or Limuru, and then leave without getting your *kipande* signed, they can put you in jail.

"Omucara asked him three different times to let him go, but he still refused. He began to get much worried because he heard that there was another man with many cows who wanted to marry this girl. Finally, when he could see that his *bwana* would not sign the *kipande*, he went to a white doctor and asked him if he would sell him some good *dowa* that would make his *bwana* sign his *kipande*. This doctor just laughed at him and said that there was no such medicine. Omucara became very discouraged and wanted to give up, but a friend of his persuaded him to go to a witch doctor."

Samwelli bit off another large piece of sugarcane and chewed it thoughtfully. "This witch doctor was a Kikuyu and lived near Nairobi. When he heard Omucara's story, he told him he would make a medicine for only six shillings, and he promised that if it didn't work he would return the money.

"The medicine he made was very powerful, for it was made out of three lizards' tails, a ball of hair taken from the stomach of a five-legged cow, and a crocodile tooth. The witch doctor cooked these things together for three days. Then he let them dry. After they had dried for seven days, he ground them into a powder while he said many powerful words. He gave the medicine to Omucara and told him to take it to the white man's house early in the morning and to put it in his coffee just before he served it.

"Omucara did all this, and the moment the white man tasted his coffee he shouted for him to come, and screamed 'Bring your labor certificate at once, and be quick about it!' Then he signed it and told him to get off his place as soon as possible and to never, never, never return.

"Omucara returned to Bunyore on the next train. He bought the necessary cows, married the girl, and now they have eleven children!"

Samwelli's eyes gleamed with triumph. "Do the white people have a medicine like that?" he demanded. I was forced to admit that as far as I knew they did not.

I related this story to Mother, but she failed to find any humor in it. "I know all about these witch doctors," she said, as she poured a cup of tea. "Right now there is a girl in the hospital who is dying. There is nothing—absolutely nothing wrong with her. But she's going to die because she thinks she has been cursed by the witch doctor."

"But you must admit that many witch doctors are very smart," I said, needling her.

"There may be intelligent ones," she conceded as she started to pour another cup of tea. "But if they are smart, it is for *their own* benefit. If you could see the condition the women are in when they come into the maternity ward, you would know all about them.

"Some day, and I hope soon, God will send us a real doctor and we'll put these old frauds out of business!" She was so carried away with this thought that she forgot how far she could tip the teapot. The lid fell off, broke the cup, and the tea spilled all over the table.

7

Mother had only been at the mission a few days when she learned that the main work of evangelism was being carried on in the villages by native pastors and evangelists. Kima was merely a center of influence, direction, instruction, and supplies. There were forty-nine congregations in all. But each congregation also operated a school for as soon as a person was converted he wanted to learn to read the lesson leaflets that were prepared at the mission. This is the reason early Christians were called "Readers."

Most of the schools were known as A schools; they took the people through what would be approximately grade two in the United States. These schools were held in the tiny mud-and-wattle church buildings that on the average seated perhaps one hundred. But scattered throughout the reserves were some advanced schools called B schools. These schools included all the curriculum of the A schools plus one higher grade. The B schools were given Government grants, the grants being paid from local native taxes. All of these better schools were required to meet in a permanent building: a structure made of stone or brick and covered with a durable roof—usually corrugated iron. Moreover, the teacher was required to have a Lower Primary Teacher's Certificate.

Providing teachers for the B schools was a major problem, for if a position were open and the mission could not provide a qualified candidate, there was a strong chance a teacher would be sent from a Government school. Since Government schools were not Christ-centered, such a teacher might even be a complete pagan.

Because of the necessity of training adequate teachers for these schools, Mother soon found herself in a classroom teaching English, geography, and arithmetic. But along with this work she made a study of the natives, noting down their problems, their customs, and the best way to improve their future.

The native churches were governed by the Church Council, made up of a minister and layman from each congregation. This council met for a *baraza* (meeting) once a month. One day a rumor spread to the mission that the native ministers were seriously considering separating themselves from the missionaries. Knowing the seriousness of the situation, Mother and Dad fasted and spent the whole night in prayer.

The tenseness of the dreaded meeting, which was held in the printing building, was finally broken by a native minister who got stiffly to his feet and said, "Bwana Ludwig-i, if one white man will steal, they will all steal." He then sat down.

Dad responded by rising and saying, "I want King George to send me a regiment of soldiers."

There was a long silence. Then the original speaker got on his feet again. "Why do you need all that protection?" he asked, the whites of his eyes wide with curiosity.

"One African killed another African five miles from here last week. If one African will commit murder, all Africans will commit murder."

The silence that followed was more intense than ever. But Mother noticed the natives had started passing notes. She prayed silently that God would have his way. Finally the spokesman stood and after noisily clearing his throat said, "A man whom God can use to answer us like that should be our chairman."

The entire council responded to this with a unanimous "*Ugh-gh-gh* [yes]."

Being chairman brought all kinds of perplexing problems. A native minister had died several years before, leaving a wife and several children. According to native law the widow became the wife of his unmarried brother. But complications had followed and so a group of natives crowded into our living room. Mother provided chairs for the men, but the women, according to custom, sat on the floor.

"Bwana," said the leader of the delegation, "you have just arrived from a Christian country where for many years your people have been helping men and women live in peace. You white people have a yesterday, a today, and a tomorrow. We only have today and tomorrow, for all our parents were heathen. Because of this we are only children in the ways of God. Many problems come up that are beyond us. I have brought this man and his wife to you so that you can give us wisdom in the matter."

Pointing to the woman on the floor, the man involved said, "This woman was my brother's wife. She loved him and bore him three children. But now that he is dead she refuses to bear even one child for me. She loves another man in our village and bore a child for him. This brings me very much sorrow, for I am her husband."

After he had finished, the wife had her turn. "Bwana and Missi Ludwig-i," she began gesturing dramatically with her right hand, "it is true that I loved my husband who died and bore him three children. He was a good man and gave me the children to bear. But this man is sterile. How can I bear him children if he doesn't give me any? He says I do not love him. He gossips about me to all the people in the village, saying that I am bad and refuse to bear his children. I determined in my heart to prove to the people that I could bear a child if I were given one to bear. I went to that man because I wanted a child, and not because I loved him or wanted to commit adultery. My husband is angry because it has been shown that he is the one who is lacking."

When she was finished she sat on the floor again and began to sob.

Dad's advice was that they should seek God's forgiveness, forgive each other, and continue to live together. This the wife was willing to do. But the husband refused. Instead he went to a witch doctor and had a rooster sacrificed in order to repair his sterilty. Then he began looking for another wife and drifted back into sin.

Many of the African pastors and evangelists were indeed remarkable men, and were much more effective in proclaiming the gospel in the villages than any missionary. They knew the old tribal stories and parables and could speak of deliverance from heathenism in very definite terms. Most of them had bodies scarred by treatments received in their pre-Christian days from the witch doctors.

One of the older ministers had a large hole in the lobe of his right ear, for the missionaries had not visited his village until he was a grown man. Some of the Kikuyu who had had the lobes of their ears stretched during their heathen days had them reduced to normal size in the mission hospitals. Others, if the hole was not too big, would hide it by turning the lobe over the top of the ear. This man, however, used the hole in his ear to an advantage in preaching.

"You should not believe anything bad about a person unless you see it with your own eyes," he would exclaim as he bugged out his enormous eyes and pointed to them with a slender finger. "And when you hear something bad about another, you should not let it go in one ear and out the other; for, if you do, it will make a mark through your head and hinder your brains." He then stretched out the ear with the hole in it. "Whenever someone tells me something bad about another Christian, I just let the words go through this hole."

Another very effective minister was Daudi Otieno, the son of the chief who had given the land to the mission. Because his father had been a respected leader, he had enormous prestige. If Mother wanted a big crowd to come to the mission, she merely had to mention it to Daudi, and the people miraculously appeared.

Mother learned a great deal about the natives from her contact with them in the school, the hospital, the *baraza*, and in counseling. But she wanted to learn as much as possible, especially about the "old ways," and so she often interviewed them, notebook in hand. One of her best sources of information was Josephu Siminkha, a leading evangelist and the son of a famous witch doctor.

Josephu would come to the mission and go into unbelievable details in relating the story of his former witchcraft practice and the experiences that led him to give it up. He had a curious habit of thrusting his face to within a few inches of the one to whom he was speaking. Unused to this, Mother would back away from him as he spoke. He responded by following to maintain the close contact with his listener. Frequently, before getting an entire episode of the "early days," she had backed around an entire circle.

"I want you to tell me how you bury your people," said Mother, as she faced him just outside the kitchen.

"I am glad you want to know about that," he replied, "because we bury all our people even though we bury some in different ways. When Bwana Wilson first came he told the people they were sinners, and they replied at once, 'We are not sinners. We bury our dead. If you want to preach to sinners, you should go to the Kikuyu and Masai. They are sinners. They throw their dead and old people out into the bushes for the hyenas to eat.'

"When a childless woman dies," he continued, taking a step forward in order to keep up with Mother who had already started to retreat, "she is buried with a sausage fruit in her arms so as to trick the evil spirits into believing that she'd had a baby."

"But what do you do with a woman who dies in childbirth?"

This subject interested her so much she forgot to back away.

"Such a woman is placed in an open grave in front of her

house in a sitting position," he replied, describing the grave with his fine, expressive hands. "When after several days the body has disintegrated sufficiently, an old woman is let down into the grave. She removes the baby with a knife and places it by the side of the corpse. The reason for this is that the baby was not born because it *refused* to be born. If a baby is allowed to be victorious in this refusal, it will persuade other babies to refuse to be born.

"All women are buried with their faces in the same direction so that if the body has to be dug up in order to kill an evil spirit that is causing a relative to be sick, the witch doctor will know whether the skeleton belonged to a man or a woman.

"A hunchback is also buried in a sitting position. But after the burial, those who helped dig the grave and fill it up, have to go to the witch doctor and pay for certain ceremonies in order that they not become hunchbacks or have hunchback children."

Heathen funerals always moved Mother deeply. I remember watching one afternoon as she stood at the edge of an unusually large funeral near the mission. Dressed in a starched white dress, she studied the scene and took notes. A wild dancer with one cheek painted red and the other white, twitched his way over to her, stamping his bell-laded feet to the rhythm of the nearby drums. Then he shook his knobkerrie right in her face. This was often done to amuse the crowd by frightening the spectator. But Mother didn't move. She didn't even see the man. Her eyes were fastened on the corpse of the young girl stretched out on a bed in front of her father's house. She felt certain that the death had been unnecessary. Oh, if she only had an adequate hospital with a dedicated white doctor!

8

Determined to see heathenism with her own eyes so she would know better how to deal with it, Mother got Abraham, one of the boys from the school, to take her to a nearby heathen village.

This eighteen-year-old lad, the eldest son of one of the early converts, led the way through the tall grass that sometimes reached to Mother's shoulders and even higher. He was armed with a Bunyore-made grass knife, a six-inch iron blade shaped like a nearly straightened question mark, and fastened by a tapering stem into a three-foot wooden handle. This *ingesu* was to protect them against snakes that might be lying in the way. A seventeen-foot python had been killed in this general area the week before.

As they threaded their way along the narrow winding path, Abraham occasionally banged the knife against a stone. This was to let any wandering leopards or hyenas know they were armed. A number of turns in the path were quite unnecessary. They were there because in former days an obstacle—an ant-hill, or a tree, or perhaps even a hut—had stood in the way. The paths were never planned, and once they existed remained unchanged.

Down in the valley, Mother stood on the bank of the tiny creek and wondered how she would cross. "Don't stand there or you'll get a fever," warned Abraham, pointing to a thick carpet of yellow-brown scum trapped in the scattered papyrus plants on the edge of the water.

He leaped lightly across the stream, dexterously managing to step in the water with only one foot. Then he quickly moved out of range from the scum. Mother, however, had to sit on a granite boulder while she took off her shoes and stockings so that she could wade across. Her nearness to the scum worried Abraham, but she felt that she was having an opportunity to prove the falseness of the old superstition; so took her time.

The heathen village on the next slope was made up of a dozen mud-and-wattle huts laid out in a crude circle. As Mother emerged through the banana trees, she noticed a line of spears and beer-stick containers by the low door of the central hut. This round affair, slightly larger and better built than the other huts, was perhaps twenty feet in diameter and stood roughly in the center of the village. This was the husband's hut; most of the others belonged to his nine wives.

A large pot of mutama beer, containing perhaps five gallons of the thin fermented gruel, rested in a little excavation near the tall cylinder-shaped grain storage building toward the west side of the open space between the huts. Some twenty people were sitting around the pot, their six- to ten-foot beer-sticks connecting them to the beer. The sticks were made of hollow reeds cleverly joined and tied together with native fiber.

As Mother watched, a series of bubbles suddenly churned to the top of the reddish liquid. When she asked the reason, one of the older men removed his stick and pointed to the cleverly woven strainer on the end. This strainer, he explained, had become clogged with bits of mutama and he had had to blow to clear it.

Among the drinkers were two little five-year-old children. Mother watched in horror as their tiny black cheeks went in and out, filling their bloated stomachs as quickly as possible. Abraham explained that the party would continue until late at night, and then the drunks, fearing a leopard or hyena, would sing ribald songs at the tops of their voices as they staggered home to their villages.

"But what will happen to the children?" she asked. Abraham seemed surprised that anyone would ask such a question, and he merely shrugged.

An old woman in a bead skirt sat beneath the eaves of one of the huts smoking an eighteen-inch pipe. A naked two-year-old boy with a chicken head dangling from his neck crouched by her side, his big liquid eyes following Mother's every move. His lips were swollen, covered with sores, and there was a heavy rash all over his body.

"What is the purpose of the chicken head?" asked Mother, stepping closer for a better view.

The old woman withdrew her pipe and spat. "He's been ill, and the witch doctor put it on to frighten the evil spirits," she replied with a gap-tooth grin.

Then she pointed to a deep, three-inch burn in his groin. "The witch doctor burned him with a red-hot knife yesterday, but the evil spirit still refuses to leave. I think the spirit of his dead mother is holding something in his stomach, for notice how swollen it is."

"You'd better take him to the hospital at Kima," said Mother, biting her tongue to keep from scolding.

"Oh, but we're not Readers. We still follow the old ways," she replied after she had spat again. "We think the witch doctor's ways are the best."

In every heathen village in Bunyore there is a small sacrificial hut furnished with three carefully chosen stones which form an altar. These brick-sized stones are arranged in a triangle just like those that support a cooking pot in each hut. It is here that the animal sacrifices are made and the meat is cooked. And it is here the spirits are supposed to dwell.

After the witch doctor has made the sacrifice and cooked the meat, he chews up choice bits and spits them in and around the altar for the spirits to enjoy. Then he gorges on the meat that is left.

While Mother was contemplating these symbols of a religion that failed to change lives, Abraham asked for permission to take her inside the main hut. Since the owner was busy with his beer, he waved them on toward the door.

As short as she was, Mother had to stoop low in order to enter. At first she couldn't see anything because of the darkness, for there was no window to let the light in and no chimney to let the smoke out. But when her eyes became accustomed to the darkness, she could see the three cooking stones in the center of the cow-dung floor and the cooking pots and storage pots on the side. A line of crude poles formed a room in the back. Here the cattle, goats, and chickens were kept. At the time it was empty, for the animals were out grazing. Another series of poles, tied horizontally to the uprights with papyrus rope, extended to the back of the hut as a shelf. Old skins and pots were stored here.

The owner's bow and arrows and a spear stood at the head of the bed by the side of the room, and the drinking gourds were at the foot. The guide picked up an arrow with a blunt head and showed it to Mother.

"This is used to get blood from a living cow," he said. "When the husband of this village gets thirsty for blood and no one kills an ox, he shoots an arrow into the neck of one of his cows, drains out a pot of blood, and then seals the vein with a wad of banana leaves. The Masai live on blood mixed with urine, milk, and ashes. But this is not our custom. Indeed, there aren't many Bunyores who use an arrow like this. Most of them get their blood at Luanda when an ox is butchered. That's why I told you about it."

Suddenly the rancid smell of the hut was too much for Mother, and she rushed outside.

"Now I want you to come to our village," said the lad, squinting up at the sun. "My mother will be making some *obusuma*, and maybe you can stay and eat with us."

The Christian village was much the same as the heathen village, except that it didn't have a heathen altar, and the open space between the huts was much cleaner. The marks of the twig brooms that had been used to sweep away the dirt and chicken droppings stood out clearly in the smooth red earth.

A new convert was building a hut on the east side of the mission station. He had found Christ a few months before in a meeting conducted by a native evangelist. Now he was breaking completely from the old life and was moving into a village where only Christians were encouraged to dwell.

He had driven a short stake into the ground, tied a ten-foot cord to it, and connected the other end to another stake, and was using it to mark the outside wall of his new house. "*Mirembe*," he shouted to Mother as he dropped his crude compass and seized her hand in both of his. "You are now seeing just the beginning of my new house. When it is finished, I want you to come and visit me."

Abraham's mother came out to greet them. She was a tall, smiling woman and her frayed Mother Hubbard was spotlessly clean. "*Mirembe, mirembe, mirembe*," she repeated as she led Mother into the hut and pointed her to a three-legged stool. "Abraham told me that you were coming, and that you would eat with us. You do not know how happy this has made us."

Mother returned the greetings. Noticing a large sore on the corner of the woman's lips, she said, "I see you have been ill."

"Yes, I was *very* ill last week. I think I stood too close to the brown scum down at the creek. Three days ago I was shaking with fever, but now the fever is gone."

She knelt behind an oblong grindstone on the freshly dunged floor and proceeded to grind some *wimbe* (finger-millet) for the *obusuma* she would soon be cooking. A handful of the tiny round grain rested on the upper end of the stone. This she skillfully pushed down three or four grains at a time and ground by rubbing them with a round, flat-sided stone which she held in both hands.

Her back and shoulders moved up and down as she worked, and Mother was surprised at the fineness of the flour and the rapidity with which it was produced. Soon a little mountain of flour formed at the bottom end of the stone. This she poured into a small cow-dung-lined basket. Then she took some more grain from a storage pot and started all over again.

As Mother watched, she hoped that pieces of the dried dung would not get into the flour. But then she reflected that even if they did, the flour would be thoroughly cooked in the boiling water and she would really only have to be concerned with her thoughts. But she knew she would have to pray to control them, for her stomach was sometimes easily turned.

"Tell me, how long have you been a Christian?" said Mother, casting her eyes about the hut which was almost identical inside to the one she had seen in the heathen village.

"I am one of the very first Christians," she replied proudly. "When I was a little girl I went to the mission to sell some eggs to Bwana Richardson. While I was there some people were singing in the old church building. I liked the music and stepped inside. There I heard about the Readers for the first time. I liked the meeting very much and kept going back. About three weeks later, I accepted Jesu Christo. Then I went to school and learned to read."

When she had finished the story, she put a pot of water on the three stones that stood in the center of the floor. Then she blew on the coals, trying to get them to flame. Failing in this, she pulled some straw from the roof just over the door and used them to get the fire started.

"What will you do when all the straw is gone from the roof?" asked Mother, noticing how skimpy it already was.

"Oh, maybe then my husband will build me a new house!"

"But won't he beat you?"

"Never, he's a Reader and has never beaten me even when I tried to iron his pants and burned a hole in them. As you know, Bunyore women don't know how to iron. When a man starts wearing pants he has to learn to iron them himself. I wish someone would teach us these things."

Suddenly the water in the pot frothed to the top. But before it could spill over the sides, she settled it by pouring in some *wimbe* flour and vigorously stirred it with a wooden paddle. Then she kept adding flour and stirring until the flour and water were solid *obusuma*. Next she ladled it onto a flat basket, and shaped it into a round mass with the paddle.

From behind her bed she produced a small pot of spinach-like green and placed it on the fire.

"I don't have any of the salt of the white people," she apologized, gesturing toward the greens. "But our salt is next best, and I know you'll like it."

Mother knew about this salt and was anxious to taste it. She had watched an old woman manufacture it by letting water trickle through a mound of grass ash. She also knew that the witch doctor used a similar ash to treat the wounds of the young men he had just circumcised. One of them had told her that it hurt even worse than the operation, and so she suspected that it was pretty strong medicine.

While the greens were heating, the woman's husband appeared with a baby girl in his arms. "This is my husband and my daughter," she said, as she pulled out a stool for him to sit on. Like Abraham, the husband was dressed in khaki shorts. He had just returned from up-country where he had been employed on a European farm in the White Highlands. The baby was completely naked, except for a tiny string around the hips. "I named her Ludwig-i, after you," beamed the mother proudly. "She was born just after you came."

When the food was ready, Abraham and his mother sat on the floor and the father handed the baby to his wife. Then Abraham passed a basin of water around and held it while each one washed his hands. After Mother had said grace, they began to eat. Abraham carefully showed Mother how to take a handful of *obusuma*, work it in the palm of her hand until it was shaped like an egg, press her thumb into the end so as to form a spoon, and then dip it into the greens.

As the family ate, they sucked loudly on the greens to assure one another they enjoyed them. The *wimbe obusuma* had a soggy, slightly bitter taste. Mother found it quite palatable. "Do you have other children?" she asked between bites.

"No, these are all that we have left," replied the father sadly. "Altogether we had twelve children, but we buried ten of them." He placed his doubled fists together to emphasize the number. "They all grew until they were about this high, and then they got sick in their chests and died." He held out the palm of his hand in a vertical position, indicating the height of a child of three. "I think the trouble was that they went too close to the brown scum on the water in the valley, for before they died they all coughed and had runny noses. My father wanted us to call the witch doctor and make a sacrifice for each one. But we refused because we are Christians."

While he was speaking, the mother chewed up some *obusuma*, carefully removed it from the healthy side of her mouth and placed it into the baby's mouth. Suddenly Mother bit down sharply on a stone and a molar which had started to cause trouble a few weeks before, began to throb. But with great determination she continued to eat and show her apprecia-tion of the family.

When the *obusuma* was gone, Abraham passed the basin around again. It still contained the same water in which they had washed their hands before they ate. Now they washed them again, carefully scraping off the *obusuma* that clung to their fingers and under their nails. Then each one sloshed their mouths full of the same water, churned it noisily through their teeth and spat it on the floor of the hut. They were careful not to spit it on any of the chicks that were hopping around looking for bits of *obusuma*.

Mother escaped filling her mouth with the water by complaining of her toothache.

Abraham offered to guide Mother home as she left, for the sun was near the horizon. "This is the time of day when the leopards are out," he exclaimed, twirling the *ingesu* in his hand.

As they started toward the mission, they passed the cattle that were being driven back to spend the night in the hut where they had just eaten. Suddenly lightning slashed across the sky and it began to rain. Quickly Abraham stepped to one side and cut several banana leaves with a deft movement of his *ingesu*. "Hold them over your head," he instructed, handing several to Mother.

While descending into the valley, Mother watched two women with fudge-colored babies in their arms as they leaped the creek, carefully avoiding the scum. Each baby had been apparently wrapped in a baby blanket. But now the babies were naked and the blankets were over the heads and around the faces of the mothers.

Mother did not know them, but as she listened to them humming, "More About Jesus," a new anger and frustration seized her. These women deserved to know more about Jesus and more about many other things as well. For a moment she didn't even feel the throb of her tooth.

9

Generally, when a new congregation sprang up and the people were ready to construct a building, a missionary was summoned to stake it out. This was because they wanted their church buildings to be square or oblong, like the buildings at Kima. Thinking of curves and circles for countless centuries had made it almost impossible for them to work in straight lines. Even when definite lines were laid out, they had a tendency to build in curves and lay walls out of plumb.

In the early forties the members of a congregation near Kima decided to build their own building without the help of a missionary. The walls were all out of line and leaned toward the center like the cone of a volcano. And since the building was made of heavy granite with very little and inadequate mortar, it was a deathtrap. Missionaries warned them of trouble to come, but they merely shrugged their shoulders.

Then on a Sunday afternoon, when the building was empty, the whole thing collapsed with a roar so loud it was heard at Kima. Fortunately, no one was hurt.

One morning Rosalyn and I went with Dad to a distant village where he had been asked to stake out a permanent stone building—something he always delighted to do. A native who had been horribly mauled by a leopard and whom Mother had nursed back to health, accompanied us, for he lived in a village along the way.

But when we came to his cluster of huts, he failed to ask us to stop. He didn't know that was necessary. He just stepped off as we drove by the path that led to his hut. He hit the red earth with a thud and rolled over several times. Horrified, Dad pulled to the side and examined him, but he was not seriously hurt.

Father chided him for not asking him to stop. "It was my first ride in a motoh-cah," he replied sheepishly. "I'll know better next time!"

When it was time to eat, we opened some canned goods and they watched our every move. "I wonder what kind of a bird laid an egg like that?" asked one after I had removed the lid from a can of beans.

"It wasn't laid by a bird!" scoffed a young man who prided himself in having more wisdom than the others. "It's a shell made out of thin iron and filled with food."

This man had been all the way to Kisumu—a distance of at least thirty miles—and thus his voice was filled with justifiable scorn as he considered the ignorance of the others.

"No, I think it's an egg," contradicted another man. He scratched the back of his neck and stared at Rosalyn while she poured the contents of the can into a paper plate.

"What kind of a bird could lay an egg that big?" demanded the man who had been to Kisumu.

"I think it was laid by one of those birds that fly overhead and go mmm-mmm-mmm like Bwana Ludwig-i's motohcah," argued the originator of the suggestion. The others nodded, indicating that they believed this was the solution to the perplexing problem.

After Father had plotted the building, and had had heavy stakes driven into the ground so that they could not be accidentally removed, he prayed with the people and headed back to Kima. But on the way we were caught in a storm and got stuck in the mud.

Getting stuck on the way to or from a native church was so common it was almost routine. Generally the rains fell in the late afternoon, and so we always tried to leave early. When Mother was along this was very difficult, for she always wanted to say another word or pray for another sick person. If we got stuck near one of our congregations, or the congregation of another group, help came at once. Dozens of natives would pour from the villages on to the road and push us out.

But sometimes when getting through was quite involved, the natives would stand nearby and make remarks that would test the metal of the most patient missionary.

"It's just the back legs that are stuck, Bwana. Why don't you make the front legs turn so that you'll get out?"

"If you'd take the shoes off the back legs, you'd get out sooner."

"Maybe the motoh-cah is tired and needs a rest."

"Look! It's angry and is spitting out of its nose just like an old woman."

But in all these comments, they were usually sincere, and Dad tried to keep that in mind. However, I remember one occasion when he got stuck near a large village and none of the people would help. There had been a rumor that some of the villagers had been making mudholes for cars to get stuck in so that they could get *baksheesh* after they had pushed them out. A light rain had been falling all that day, and it was drizzling when we got stuck; but Father didn't think the rain had been heavy enough to produce those slippery ruts. Moreover, a great number of people showed up the moment his wheels began to spin.

When he asked them to push, they extended their palms and with broad grins replied, "We'll push you out when you fill our hands with *baksheesh*."

But Dad was in no mood to pay anyone. He got out, rolled up his sleeves, put on the chains, and within a few minutes got through the mud. He drove down the road until he came to a solid place and stopped. Then he motioned for the natives to come and waited until they had gathered around him.

Soon a hundred or more were standing by the car, wondering what he had in mind. It so happened that he had a *debi* half full of one-cent, five-cent and ten-cent pieces. He had picked this money up from one of the congregations and was taking it to the mission for safe keeping.

While they waited, he poured the money in a heap on the ground before them. Then he scooped it up and let it run through his fingers. The natives looked at the miniature mountains of copper and licked their lips. He waited until all their eyes were focused on the money, and then, without saying a word, tossed it back in the *debi* and drove off.

He knew that the story of his dramatic visual aid would be repeated throughout the villages for years, and that it would be used in many a pastor's sermon. But his main hope was that they had learned a lesson.

On our return we found Mother sitting at a desk. Her eyes were ablaze and rimmed in red from weeping. Her thick, black fountain pen rested in the fingers of her right hand like a mortar that had been tossing shells at the enemy for the last dozen hours. "I just talked to one of the elders about starting a boarding school for girls," she said, pointing to a stack of envelopes addressed to friends in America. "And do you know what he told me?" She paused dramatically, her lips in a grim line. We waited spellbound to hear what the unfortunate man had said.

"That elder, that father, that husband, that preacher told me that we should not educate the women, for if we did so they would know as much as the men and then the husbands wouldn't be able to keep their positions as the head of the house!

"By the time I got through with him, he had decided that he would think twice before he ever said such a thing again. The very idea."

"Well, what are you going to do about it?" asked Dad, counting the envelopes and making a mental calculation of the amount of postage that would be required.

"I'll tell you what I'm going to do," she replied, giving the edge of the table a series of resounding whacks with her tightly doubled fist. "I'm going to pray that he won't be able to sleep until he changes his mind. And I've written to all these people in America and have asked them to pray that God will give us a girls' school where we can train the girls to be *real* mothers in the New Africa. And I know that we'll have such a school, for our God is able. I've written to the secretary of the Missionary Board, and I know he'll help us."

She picked up a sheet of paper and was in the act of addressing it when she suddenly looked up at Dad and said, "The pitiful thing is that it takes a letter a month to six weeks to get to America and that it will be from three to four months before I can get a reply. But I know that God is speaking to the people and the Board right *now!*"

From that day on, the moment Mother awakened in the morning she remained stretched out in bed while she prayed from a half hour to an hour. She always prayed out loud, for she was very conscious of the near presence of the One who had healed her. And always included in that prayer was the plea that a method be provided to educate the women of Kenya.

10

Early in the spring, just after a short, heavy rain, Samwelli called and asked if I would like to make a trap and eat some flying ants with him. Gladys had been enthusiastic about them, and so I answered that I would be right out.

He led me to a place just a few yards from our home and pointed to some tiny holes in the red, flat earth. "There are lots of ants here," he said, licking his lips with the confidence of an experienced ant trap builder. "All we have to do is to build a trap and our stomachs will be full!"

We got dozens of long, slender sticks and built a low basin-shaped framework over the holes. Then, while Samwelli dug in front of the framework a deep hole about the size and shape of a candy bucket, I went to the house and asked Mother for an old blanket. Samwelli used the blanket to cover the framework. He took special care to make sure the structure was camera-tight except for a small opening over the hole which he lined with banana leaves.

"The ants will come now," he said, licking his lips and patting his stomach with anticipation. "They will follow the light and fall into the hole. The slippery banana leaves on the side will stop them from crawling out."

Presently a white line of ants started to tumble in the hole. Samwelli picked up a handful and stuffed them in his mouth, smacking his lips loudly. Not to be outdone, I gingerly picked one up. But before I ate it, I held it up to the light for examination. The zebra-striped body was about a quarter of an inch in length and was equipped with inch-long, transparent wings. Feeling Samwelli's eyes on me, I clenched my fists, gulped, popped it into my mouth, and started to chew.

Samwelli shook with laughter. "Don't eat them one at a time," he instructed. "You don't eat beans or corn that way. You must eat a handful at once!" I hesitated, but Samwelli smacked his lips so loudly I reasoned that they must be good. So, I reached into the bottom of the hole and quickly pushed a hundred or so of the squirming things into my mouth all at once and furiously began to chew so that none could escape.

To my utter amazement, I found that they were unusually delicious with a greasy, peanut-like flavor.* From then on I was a confirmed anteater. The ants didn't fill the vacuum caused by the lack of catsup, hot dogs, candy, and ice-cream cones, but they helped.

There were times, however, when Samwelli and I got hungry for ants and there was no obliging rain to bring them out. On such occasions we would build a trap anyway, and then pound rocks together by the entrance to make the ants think it was raining. Sometimes the ants responded, but more often than not, it was wasted effort.

While we were eating the ants, Haabwe and Neva came over to join us. Ant gourmets for many years, they crammed them into their mouths the moment they waddled through the door. Haabwe was eating them as fast as she could snatch them up, when suddenly she stopped, a question mark on her pocked face. "Maybe Mama would like some," she said, a couple of wings hanging from the side of her mouth. "Let me go and ask."

I didn't believe Mother would even taste one, and I was right. But Haabwe persisted. "They are very good, Mama," she pled. "Let me fill a handkerchief full for you. *Cupa cupa* [yum yum]!"

"But I c-couldn't eat them a-alive," she exclaimed, lifting her hands in horror.

"Then I'll fry you some!" said Haabwe. And before Mother could protest, she vanished.

Haabwe spread her hands over the hole in front of the trap so that no one could get a single ant until a good amount had been accumulated for Mother. When the hole was half full, she placed them in a clean, white handkerchief, and tied the four ends together in a heavy knot.

———

*Once, the day after I had told an American elementary school that ants taste like peanuts, a fifth-grader stopped me on the street. "Ants don't taste like peanuts!" he said, an accusing look on his freckled face. "How do you know?" I asked. He then confessed that he had eaten some red ants! There is a difference—a big difference!

"I don't think Mother will eat them, even if they are fried," I ventured.

"Oh, yes she will," replied Haabwe, rolling her eyes and moistening her lips. "The only thing that tastes better than fried ants with grains of salt on them is fried locusts." She patted her stomach as she spoke of locusts, and her eyes had a knowing gleam that lit up her whole face.

The moment Haabwe left to prepare the ants for Mother, Neva and Samwelli went after the seemingly exhaustless stream that flowed in a solid line from the trap. They reminded one of Ripley's never-ending column of Chinese. Haabwe and Samwelli went after them with both hands. While one hand was jamming the squirming things into their mouths, the other hand was pinching up more. They crunched them down as if they were starving. When I teased them about it, Samwelli replied, "Flying ants are to us what *caki* is to you—only flying ants are much, much better!"

Both Samwelli and Neva had a little fingernail-sized scar in the center of their foreheads, and one on the top of each wrist and above both knees. Having been curious about these scars for a long time, I asked Samwelli to explain.

"Many years ago," he said, speaking around a mouthful of ants, "We had a lot of smallpox,* and thousands of people died. The witch doctors knew that if a person had the disease he would never get it again, and so they cut the people on their foreheads, on each wrist, and above each knee. Then they put fluid from the disease into each of the wounds. This saved a lot of lives."

He got so interested in telling me about this, he didn't keep his lips closed as tightly as he should have, and a number of ants squirmed across the barrier of his teeth toward safety. He recaptured several of them with a snakelike motion of his tongue, but one or two managed to get across his lips and fly away.

"The witch doctor who cut me was a very stern old man," he continued. "If I moved or even groaned while he was cutting

---

*This was the severe epidemic of 1916 that brought death to hundreds of thousands throughout Kenya.

a cross into my flesh he picked up a grain of corn and then flipped it into my wound with his fingers—and they were very powerful. Father paid him a rooster for his work. The witch doctors in those days ate a lot of money, and some of them had twenty or even eighteen wives. I know—"

"Look who's coming!" exclaimed Neva, pointing with her lips toward the wild olive tree where the missionaries buried their dead. I turned my head and saw a light-skinned young man of about twenty-five cautiously following the puddle-drenched path that led to our house. He had taken off his shoes to save them from the mud, and was carrying them on his head. There was a bright red cloth between them and his magnificently combed hair, and the edges fluttered in the evening breeze. His hair parted in a deep part on the left, was strictly European, and its appearance was the result of long, happy minutes with a homemade wooden comb in front of a cracked mirror he had brought back from the big city.

"Who is he?" I asked.

"Oh, that's Oriedo," replied Samwelli, flashing his dazzling teeth in a wide smile. "He's just returned from Nairobi where he worked for a white man. I think he has his eyes on Haabwe."

Neva scrambled to her feet and headed for the kitchen. "I'd better warn Haabwe that he's coming," she said over her shoulder. "A man who has been eating shillings in Nairobi and who wears shoes isn't found every day!"

Feeling that something terribly exciting was about to happen, I followed Neva to the kitchen. "Oriedo is coming!" she said in a loud whisper. "And I think he wants to speak to you!"

Haabwe stuck out her pointed, red tongue in a look of surprise. "What shall I do?" she demanded, blushing a deep black and pushing the pan of ants off the burner.

"Give me a basin of water for him to wash his feet in," said Neva hurriedly. "I'll keep him outside until you're ready."

Haabwe filled one of Mother's best cake pans with water and hurriedly thrust it at Neva, thus splashing a few drops on the floor. "Now don't let him come until I'm ready!" she said. "I'll let you know with a loud cough."

84

Then she took a generous pat of lard and rubbed it on her freshly shaved head, making it glisten and shine. Next, she rubbed some more on her legs and massaged her shins with practiced strokes until they were like polished boots.

This done to her satisfaction, she smoothed out her white, cotton dress and coughed.

Neva opened the door and Oriedo stepped inside the kitchen. His brown shoes were tied in even bows, and his red, knitted stockings with their inch-spaced flutings were turned down just below the knee. His khaki shorts and matching jumper were razor-sharp. Haabwe gasped at the sight of his magnificence. But quickly remembering her proper roll in such a situation, she scowled as if she had been insulted.

Feeling that I was disturbing something, I said, "When are you going to take the fried ants in to Mother?"

"They are ready now," she replied, motioning toward the pan. "Why don't *you* take them in?"

I took them in and placed them on Mother's desk. "Taste some," I said, "Haabwe fried them for you, and they smell very good."

Mother looked up from her writing. She pointed at me with her large, black fountain pen, its nib blunted from the writing of thousands of pages, and said, "Charles, I don't want any." She spoke with her mind on something else.

"But how can you understand the natives if you don't eat their food?" I argued.

My argument went home, and she picked up four or five ants and slowly ate them. Then she pushed the pan away. "You'll have to leave me now," she said, "I'm busy!"

I took the ants back to the kitchen. "Mother doesn't want any more," I said.

Haabwe and Oriedo were sitting across the table from one another, and so I thrust the ants between them. I stood and watched as they ate and wondered what it was like to be in love.

Outside, the moon was a thin sickle in the sky, and I could hear a very faint howl of a hyena. Finally Neva said to me,

"Bwana Charles—I, don't you think it's time for you to go into the house with your parents?"

I didn't think it was. I knew something mysterious was happening, and I didn't want to miss any of it. But it was plain that these mysterious things would get along better if I left the kitchen. And so I stuffed my mouth with ants and departed.

Just before I went to bed Dad came into my room and said, "Miss Baker is going to be back in about a month. This means that we're going to have to start moving tomorrow. We'll be moving into the laundry on the east side of the mission. You'd better stay around the mission so that I can get hold of you when you're needed."

11

In some ways the building that had been built for a laundry, although it had never been used for that purpose, was much better than the house we had been living in. For one thing it was built of stone and had the unusual luxury of a cement floor. This meant that we didn't have to move all the furniture periodically and put down a fresh coat of cow dung. Also, there were rooms for all of us. But there was no kitchen, and so Dad decided he would build one. Feeling there was no time to waste, he set to work at once. Mr. Kramer had burned a large kiln of brick nearby, and one of my jobs was to help carry brick for the new building.

I carried the bricks in my arms until the native women taught me that it was much simpler to carry them on my head.

Dad had never laid a brick in his life, but he had books on the subject and was soon handling a trowel like an expert. He employed an odd assortment of men to carry brick and mortar and to do other necessary errands. As the tiny building neared completion, he hired a Luo to help put on the roof.

Mother was amused that he would hire this man, for he wasn't very big and he only wore a goatskin. But he had assets Mother didn't recognize. Dad had noticed a series of perhaps a dozen holes around the rim of each ear; I was told that each hole represented a cow he owned. This man was also light on his feet and rather agile; so Dad used him to climb up on the sisal-pole scaffold and hand him nails and sheets of corrugated iron as he needed them.

The wizened old fellow filled the holes in his ears with nails and thus had the free use of his hands. When Dad needed another nail he pulled it out of his ear. The old man—I never learned his name—didn't think this was funny at all. As far as he was concerned, it was just the thing to do. He was very efficient.

Both Dad and Mother hated to see anything wasted and despised a loafer regardless of his color. When it came time to fix the road that led from the main mission house to the laundry, Dad employed about thirty men to carry sandy grayish-like murum from the valley just below. He watched them as they worked and made up his mind that they were taking advantage of him. Never once did any of them manage to fill a single barrel in one day.

He sent his foreman to call them to his office so that he could have a *shauri* (conference) with them. In almost no time they came trooping in, their faces hacked with toothy smiles, for there is nothing a Bunyore likes more than to have a *shauri* —especially if he can have it with the *Bwana Mukubwa* (Big Boss).

"Boys, I have a new custom I want to explain to you," said Dad, stroking his chin wisely. "I'm going to tell you how you can get your work done long before the four o'clock drum beats in the afternoon. This new way of mine will enable you to get your tickets* marked so that you can go to the gardens and oversee your wives long before the sun reaches the top of the sky."

"Oh-ho, oh-ho?" they questioned, shaking their heads in disbelief.

——
*A ticket was a postcard-sized piece of cardboard with thirty squares marked on it. At the end of each day's work an X was marked into a square by the foreman. A filled card was exchanged for a month's wages—$1.50—according to the exchange at that time.

"Now, I know you have great strength," continued Dad. "I have seen how much murum you can carry when you are carrying it for yourselves. I have a promise to make which I know you will like. When you have carried three barrels of murum, you can go home even if its only eight o'clock in the morning."

"Too much, too much!" murmured Gasoline, shaking his head in dismayed sorrow. "We can't do it—it would kill us!"

"It's impossible to kill strong men like you," replied Dad with a grin.

They haggled for a bit, and then slowly nodded their heads. "We'll try," said Wheelbarrow.

"But if it kills us," added Cementi, "you'll have to take us to the hospital."

The next morning we began to hear noises at sunrise. I hurried out to see what was going on. Some of the barrels were already half full. The men rushed back and forth as if the witch doctor had placed a curse on them. The pans on their heads were loaded to the brim, and the murum slopped over on their naked shoulders. And where before they had stopped to greet and shake hands with one another each time they passed, now they hurried by their friends as if they were mortal enemies. Some of them nearly ran, so eager were they to get their barrels filled. It was amazing to see their concentrated industry. Lazy Man and Wheelbarrow worked so furiously their faces were drenched with sweat. All of them, including Gasoline, were through by ten o'clock in the morning.

Whenever anyone asked why they were working so hard, they replied proudly and with great dignity, "We're working on contract-i!" After this, three barrels of murum was considered a day's work.

We were in the act of moving when a middle-aged man dressed in an extremely ragged and dirty loincloth came to Dad with an unusual request. He wanted his hair cut!

"Why don't you get your friends to cut it?" asked Dad.

"I don't have any friends," he replied rolling his big eyes mysteriously.

"Surely you know someone who would cut it," persisted Dad.

"No one will even come close to me," he replied sadly. "You're my only friend!"

As he spoke it was evident that his mind had known better days, and we knew this was the reason no one would cut his hair. The Bunyores have an acute fear of the insane.

Dad asked him to sit on a log while he got his clippers. Unfortunately, the clippers did little good. His course hair was matted and filled with sand. Trying to cut it with hand clippers was like trying to clear a path in the jungle with a razor blade. Finally Dad put the clippers down and got some sheep shears, and they did the job.

When he was finished the man pointed to his feet. "Bwana," he pled hopefully, "please take the jiggers out. No one else will help me."

His feet were so loaded with these pests they were twisted outward at a forty-five degree angle. Dad asked Haabwe to bring a bucket of hot water. Then he poured some jaze into it and had Akhabwaba—this was his name—soak his feet in the solution. Then Dad went about his business and forgot that he had a patient waiting.

Four hours later, when he remembered, he came back with a needle and picked out hundreds and hundreds of the flea-like intruders. Many of them had already built pea-sized bags, and these grayish bags were bursting with more jiggers which, if left alone, would repeat the terrible process.

Jiggers—the name Dad gave him, for the other was too difficult to pronounce—was so happy someone paid attention to him and cared for his needs, he announced happily that Dad was his father. He stayed around the mission until all his jiggers had been removed and burned. Then he returned to his nearby village and became a regular attendant at the church services. But every time he needed a haircut, he came to the mission and Dad cut it for him.

Soon other mentally unbalanced men came in for the white man's help. Many of these unfortunates along with their long hair—generally filled with string and feathers—had crude manacles forged onto their wrists by native blacksmiths to protect the terrified population.

Infection had set in the wrist of one of these men, and the flesh had swollen around the iron manacle until it was at least two inches below the surface. His wrist was like a tree that had had a heavy, tight wire tied around it as a sapling. It crawled with infection.

As Dad led him to the workshop to remove the manacle, a native warned, "Bwana Ludwig-i, he is a very crazy man. And if you take off the manacle, he may kill someone, and it will take at least forty men to catch him."

But Dad was more afraid of blood poisoning, and so he fastened the manacle in a vice and with a hacksaw and cold chisel pried it off. As predicted, the man ran away. But we went after him in our lorry and he surrendered with just a little coaxing. Dad arranged for him to be sent to an asylum in Nairobi.

The morning after our first night in the laundry, a man was carried into the hospital who had a deep, three-inch gash on the top of his bald head. As I looked at him it seemed to me that I had seen him before. I mentioned this to Jairo, and he said to me quietly so as not to be overheard, "His name is Onyamba. He was here last month with his wife whom he had beaten up. She almost died."

Onyamba had two wives, and he was in the habit of beating them up at the slightest provocation. "What happened to you?" I asked.

"My wife hit me over the head with a *jembe*."

"But how did she do it?" I asked, teasing him and feeling his heavy biceps.

"Both women got together!" he replied, hanging his head and grinning foolishly.

Mother washed his wound with raw alcohol, and as it flowed into the cut that reached to the skull, I gritted my teeth. Then she got a surgical needle and thread and sewed him up, making a dozen stitches in all.

90

After it was all over and we were on our way home, I said, "Mother, you tried to hurt him just a little extra didn't you?"

"No, I didn't," she said, "but maybe he'll behave himself from now on!"

"But you were glad that it hurt," I persisted, "weren't you?"

Mother didn't answer, but I could see a gleam in her brown eye and blue eye and the corners of her lips turned up slightly.

12

Even though there were no telephones, the news that the Prince of Wales would visit Kisumu spread throughout the country within a few hours. The moment Mother heard it, she looked at Rosalyn and me and announced that we were going down to see him.

"If we go, we'll have to leave here at about four in the morning," warned Dad, "for the ship he's on will dock at Kisumu at about seven."

"That's all right," interrupted Mother. "Getting to see the future king of England is part of the children's education. It isn't everyone who gets to see the Prince of Wales!"

Mother decided that I should be dressed in my very best, and so she summoned Kefa and told him to iron my pants. That is she meant to tell him to *iron* them. Instead, she told him that he should *burn* them. When he objected she went after him furiously and told him to do what she said without any questions. Her patience with natives who would wash the dishes and not sweep the floor had run out long ago. She decided to crack down, and this was a good beginning.

Obediently, Kefa thrust my best pants into the stove, and the next morning when I groped for them in the dark they were not to be found. Mother was then forced to compromise her conscience and allow me to wear my second-best pair.

Dawn was just breaking as our lorry shuddered down the rough escarpment toward the city. But there was just enough light for Mother to see a smudge of dirt on my cheek. "Charles, your face is dirty," she exclaimed. "We can't let you meet the Prince of Wales looking like that! He'll think we're heathen!"

I tried to rub it off, but without success. Mother, however, was determined. Not being able to find any water, she moistened a handkerchief with her tongue and rubbed it off with that.

"What are you, a cat?" asked Dad, swerving quickly to the left to avoid an antbear hole.

"But, John, we're going to see the Prince of Wales!"

By the time we arrived at the dock, where the ship bearing the royal passenger would drop anchor, nearly the entire white population of the city and neighboring missions had appeared. This group of from thirty to fifty had come in their Sunday best. Their helmets were freshly blocked and their shoes glistened in the light of the fierce morning sun that splashed in Lake Victoria just beyond them.

Ever since the death of Horace—the eccentric hippo who used to prowl the streets at night and take an occasional nap on the steps of the bank—Kisumu had been a dull place. Old-timers spoke wistfully of the exciting days when the Chief of Police, Major Foran, had burned the Mohammedan Mosque in order to kill its huge colony of rats that were known to be hosts to bubonic plague-infested fleas. But since those colorful times, the most interesting news was concerned with who had malaria or blackwater fever, or whose cook had turned out to be a thief.

Kisumu took advantage of the day. Local chiefs arrayed themselves in their finest and brought along all their carefully polished and smiling wives; the witch doctors dressed their parts, wearing hippo-teeth crowns, big collections of various-shaped gourds, belts loaded with knives, and heavy strings of charms. Each medicine man tried to outdo his rival. And thousands of other natives poured into the dock area to see the distinguished eldest "son of the Sultan." A favorite native costume was a huge, enormously heavy, leather hat fringed with dozens of full-length ostrich feathers.

Fifty or sixty members of the King's African Rifles stood at

92

attention, their long-stocked World War I rifles at their sides. They were dressed in razor-sharp khaki shorts, heavy blue sweaters, and there were blue puttees around their bare legs. Their heels and the sides of their feet were as white as scouring stones could make them. Standing on their heads like cone-shaped tumblers were their smart red fezzes—the special pride of each man. These fezzes were carefully pressed slightly forward like the Leaning Tower of Pisa, and the long black tassels were strictly on the left.

As the red-bottomed ship steamed into port on its trip from Uganda, some of the Englishmen, their hearts back in Piccadilly Circus, touched handkerchiefs to their eyes. The Prince, flanked on either side with British guards dressed in white, stood at the rail of the ship and waved at us with a boyish hand.

While the ship moved into place, an expensive aisle rug was rolled out for His Royal Highness to walk on. But when the Prince saw it, he sent word that he would not get off the ship until the rug was removed. "I will walk on the cement like anyone else," he announced.

The rug was quickly disposed of, and in a moment he strode lightly down the steps and shook hands with each of us. Dressed in a salt and pepper suit, and a warm smile, he made a great impression. I remember he asked Dad what he was doing and how he liked the country.

When it was my turn to go up to him and take his hand, there was a cold terror in my stomach, for I remembered the rapturous way Rosalyn had described him to me on our way to Kisumu. "His father, George V, is the most famous man in the world. The sun never sets on his empire. The Prince of Wales will be known as His Majesty King Edward VIII, by the Grace of God, of Great Britain, Ireland, and the British Dominions beyond the Seas, King, Defender of the Faith, Emperor of India." But Mother gave me a shove forward, and since a thousand mile journey starts with one step, I was soon marching forward to the dapper young man who was soon to be loaded with such glorious titles. One of the stiff white guards, standing at attention by his side, lifted his sword several inches from its scabbord as I approached, and my heart went up with it.

Having strong memories of the Tower of London, I hoped I wasn't about to suffer the fate of Anne Boleyn. But my fears were for nothing. His Royal Highness shook my hand, and I retreated to my mother with the sense of accomplishment that King Arthur must have felt when Excaliber leaped into his hand.

During all of this time, a hornet sat on the pinnacle of the future king's helmet. Occasionally, as the royal head moved, it would fly away and circle around like a British fighter at Gibraltar. But it always returned to the starting point.

After everyone shook hands with him, we all joined in singing "For He's a Jolly Good Fellow." Then His Royal Highness thanked us with a gesture of his hand and was whisked away in a black limousine to the home of a wealthy businessman.

Since it was still early in the morning, Dad decided he had enough time to transact some business and get home before it rained. Part of that business was for me to be measured for a new pair of shoes. He let me off at his favorite shoe store and then headed for the post office, for Mother was eager to see if she had a reply from the Board in regard to her proposed Girls' School.

Ready-made shoes were an almost unheard of item in the Colony. Four or five slender Hindus were sitting on the fiber-matted floor as I entered. They were surrounded with stacks of leather, nails, spools of thread, cans of paste, and old Indian newspapers. Each one was busy with his particular contribution to the manufacture of footwear. Working with both their feet and hands, they were marvelously efficient. The shoes seemed to take shape and grow in their midst like rabbits in the hands of magicians.

Taking a last puff on the roll-your-own cigarette, the head of the firm adjusted his loose-fitting *dhoti*, got out his account book, and asked me to place my bare, right foot on an empty page. Then he carefully outlined it with a stubby, yellow pencil.

Next, he produced several styles of shoes and asked which

kind he should make and what the color should be. I chose a brown number with a high, blunt toe, for I thought it would be useful in playing football. He made a notation of these requirements just below the outline of my foot in his own, native writing; and then, while he stroked his eyebrow-sized moustaches, said, "They'll be ready in one month."

As I waited in the store for Father's return, I noticed the pictures on the wall. There was, of course, the usual picture of Ghandi in his loincloth. In addition, there were a number of grotesque, and full-color portraits of their gods. The picture that most intrigued me was of a fat well-dressed man sitting on a throne with his feet on an elaborate footstool. A young lady was lying on her back across his knees, and he, with his claw-like fingers deep in her bare abdomen, was pulling her apart while the blood spurted.

Just as the smell of garlic began to drift in from the apartment in the rear, Father appeared. "Did Mother get a letter from the Board about the Girls' School?" I asked anxiously, for the Girls' School project had become a family affair owing, I suppose, to constant repetition.

"Nothing yet," answered Dad, leading the way up to a Goanese store at the top of the block. This store, one of the better ones in Kisumu, was made of poured cement and carried a supply of canned goods and, unfortunately for me, a dark array of mysterious medicines designed to bring health and vitality to small malaria-racked boys from America.

One of the dark medicine bottles that caught Mother's eyes was a concoction of iron, quinine, epsom salts, and a few other unpalatable things I have forgotten. This was just the medicine I needed, she decided. Since the grisly label said three teaspoonfuls a day, that was my sentence and it was not subject to appeal.

This vile essence of evil tasted like concentrated rabbit gall, and whenever the clock chimed 10:00 A.M., 12:00 noon, and 4:00 P.M., I felt like a condemned man listening to curfew at dawn on the final day after the scaffold had been constructed and the noose with its thirteen knots had been prepared.

As I entered the store with Dad, I noticed a fresh supply of genuine American catsup on the sprawling counter in the center of the building. I went over to the glass case and lovingly picked up one of the half dozen bottles, and when I was certain that Dad was watching, turned it in my hands and licked my lips. Dad got the hint and asked the price.

"The price is only three shillings," replied the proprietor, gently wiping the bottles with a feather duster. But three shillings was seventy-five American cents. This was a huge bite from a missionary's slender allowance, and so Dad lost interest at once. Mother made several purchases, and while the carry-out boy was taking them to the car, we went down to the Mohammed Ali *dukah* for a bottle of soda.

The plump Mohammed was in a good mood when we came in, and so he treated us all to a bottle of rose. This time Mother didn't shudder when he thrust the dusty neck of the bottle into the glasses to control the foam, or even when he wiped the tall tumblers with his shirttail.

While we were enjoying our drinks, a missionary from the Pentecostal mission joined us. Soon the conversation drifted to the foundations of the big church at Kima. "When that building was started," he said, "I felt that it was too big. I hope you can finish it, but I have my doubts. The rains aren't doing those exposed brick any good. You know these homemade Kenya brick aren't as good as the brick we get in the States."

Mother knew that what he and others had said was probably true, but she had faith that through some miracle the money would be provided and the building completed.

As we rounded the big curve by Old Kisumu, Dad pointed to the *dukahs* that were being dismantled. "I understand the corrugated iron is being sold at auction," he said with anticipation, for he loved auctions, "and when it is, I'll be there. Some of that iron could be used in the Girls' School buildings."

Fortunately for us, it hadn't rained that day, and when we came to the *T* in the road beyond Maseno, the sky in the west was all clear. And so, instead of turning to the right on the road that led to Kima, we continued on to the native mar-

Top: A big capture in East Africa. Lower left: Some of Mrs. Ludwig's girls learn arithmetic. Lower right: Mrs. Ludwig, assistants, and patient in front of a dispensary.

Upper left: One of Twyla Ludwig's earliest pictures. Upper right: Her wedding picture. Bottom: A picture of the Ludwigs after they had served several years in Africa.

ket at Luanda. Mother wanted some meat, and this was the time to get it.

The market, covering perhaps three acres of ground, was surrounded with a high fence made of a combination of thorn trees, oleanders, and sisal plants. The hard bare earth of the market was occupied by hundreds of small businessmen and women who sat on the ground with their wares around them.

One of the women was selling small packages of rock salt. The packages were made of deftly-wrapped banana leaves and contained approximately two tablespoons of low-grade salt. Each square package sold for about one and a half American cents. But always before a sale could be concluded, there were several pleasant moments of haggling during which both parties puffed on their foul-smelling pipes. Next to this woman there was another older woman who dealt in *ebisindu* (quails).

A large, flat dung-lined basket by her side was filled with the little brown speckled birds. They didn't struggle or try to get away, and since their legs were not tied I was curious. Examinations showed that their wings and legs had been snapped. When Mother learned this, a tenseness crossed her face, for she loved birds and animals and despised all cruelty.

Next to the crippled birds were bell-shaped, papyrus-rope baskets filled with singers. The birds that sang were carefully fed and were used to entice other quail into the many traps that dotted the countryside. I listened while sales were made and found that an ordinary quail was sold for six Kenya cents while a singer brought double that amount.

But since we had come for meat and it was getting late, we hurried by the pipe and tobacco and snuff sellers, and the pot venders, the dealers in chickens and eggs, corn and dried fish, and beer sticks and beads, and went over to the place where the cows were butchered.

Most of the meat had been sold at the place where we stopped, but there was still a part of a leg of beef hanging in the center of a tripod made of sisal poles. With her hands, Mother indicated the size of the piece of meat she wanted. Nodding that he understood, the native, dressed in a blood-smeared pair of khaki shorts, cut at the meat with his knife. But the knife was exceedingly dull and merely forced the meat away. He tried two or three times again, but without success. Then, with an obscene oath, he held the meat against one of the poles with his bare foot and slashed out the necessary amount by holding the knife in both hands.

Mother, however, didn't like the price, the meat, and the way he cut it. She shook her head.

The man next to this one was in the process of butchering a young bull, and she decided to wait for him. This way the meat would be fresh, and she could get a choice bit from the hump.

A large crowd had gathered, and the black animal that was about to be killed was lying on the ground. Its feet were bunched and tied together with leather thongs. A native Mohammedan made the sign of Islam, and the butcher pressed the sharp points of the bull's horns into the ground so that it couldn't turn its head. Then, while he held it in position by its jaws, he signaled that it was time to cut its throat.

The actual killing was done by a Muslim so that the followers of the Prophet would not refuse to buy the meat. The clever butcher knew that the killer or his method made no difference to the heathen or the Christians. The Muslim wrapped a turban around his head and started to cut the bull's throat. But this was a tedious job because it was a Brahman and had an extremely wide brisket. As he neared the actual throat, an old man brought a large black pot and held it in readiness to catch the blood. And when the blood spurted he filled it to the brim. Then he moved away so that others could fill their containers. Some of the blood spilled on the ground, and an old man scooped it up with his palms and sucked it noisily.

When the head had been severed and twisted away, it was sold to a woman who carried it off by the horns. Then the body was opened and the entrails taken out. The stomach was slit and some of the men cut long slivers of meat which they swished around in the juices and semidigested food. These they ate raw, smacking their lips loudly and rubbing their naked stomachs to show that it was good.

After the skin had been pegged on the ground to dry so that it could be sold to a Somali who dealt in animal hides, teen-age boys crawled onto it and sliced off bits of fat and meat. These, they ate raw. When the piece was large, they held it in their teeth while they cut off a chewable section with a knife or sharp piece of bamboo. From a distance it seemed that they were severing their tongues.

A number of witch doctors stood by, waiting for certain glands to be used in their medicines. And chicken hawks circled a few feet above, looking for an opportunity to swoop down and steal a piece of flesh. Occasionally a greedy hawk, its fierce yellow eyes cunningly watching, would whiz over a native and with an unexpected dive grab a piece of meat from the wide basket on top of her head. Then with the prize safe in its needle-sharp black talons, it would circle higher and lazily float around in ever-widening circles while it nibbled on the meat in much the same manner as an American nibbles on an ice-cream bar.

Mother got her piece of meat from the hump, and we all returned to the car to leave for home. But before Dad let the clutch in, an old man, bent forward like an open safety pin, came to the window and held out a clawlike hand for a gift. His backbone had been broken in the small of his back, and when he moved I could see the fractured end moving under his skin. It was a revolting sight. Dad slipped a ten-cent piece into his hand and then drove off.

As we approached the mission, I suddenly said something I had been thinking all day, but up to then had not had the courage to say. "You know the Prince of Wales may be a very great man, but I know something he doesn't know."

"What could that be?" asked Rosalyn with an obvious sniff, for she still tingled with the excitement of meeting and shaking hands with such an important person.

"I know about the hornet that sat on his helmet," I replied triumphantly. "I watched it all the time he was there speaking to the people, and I know he didn't know anything about it!"

There was a long pause in the stream of conversation after this weighty statement. Then Mother broke the silence by gravely saying, "Charles, you have learned a lesson—a very great lesson. *Never* forget it!" As she said this, a sense of relief crossed her face, and I knew that she knew that I was getting a unique education.

We ate the meat that night, for we, like all the other white people, had no refrigeration and we didn't like to eat the meat after it had spoiled even though the natives preferred it that way.

13

"Mama, you must help me," sobbed Haabwe almost hysterically, hot tears cascading down her pitted face and dropping on our living room floor.

"What has happened? Did your father die?" asked Mother, pausing in her writing and motioning for her to be seated.

"It's much worse than that," she replied, shaking her head and politely ignoring the seat.

Mother knew how the Africans loved to talk about all kinds of unrelated things before getting down to the point of concern, and since her desk was piled high, she said, "Tell me your main trouble at once. Maybe I can help you."

"It's about my marriage," she began. Then she became so convulsed with grief she couldn't speak. Biting her lip, she wrestled with her emotions until she had them partly under control, and then she continued brokenly, "As you may have guessed from his many visits, Oriedo wants to marry me. But my father won't let him."

"Why won't he let him?" asked Mother, deeply concerned, for she had been following the romance with a definite interest.

"Because—because Oriedo only has three cows, and Father says that he must have seven cows, four goats, and twenty-four shillings."

"Well, that isn't a big problem," answered Mother with a smile. "Oriedo is a smart young man. He can go to Nairobi again and earn enough money to buy some more cows, and then you can get married. Only I do hope that he will become a Christian before you get married, for I would like you and him to be a part of the New Africa."

"But my father won't wait," she replied. Then she broke into a long fit of crying.

After her flood of tears had ebbed, Mother asked gently, "Why won't he wait?"

"Because there is an old man who wants to marry me and he has seven cows. But, Mama, he already has three wives; and he's ugly and he beats his wives for the least little thing. I want to have a Christian home, and I know God doesn't want me to live with a man who has other wives."

Mother knew what marriage and polygamy in Bunyore meant, for she was making a thorough study of it by constantly questioning the women in the hospital. Years later, she wrote a chapter on the subject:

"Girls are trained from the day they are born for marriage. They must be hardened into servitude, and beautified. . . .

"When the mother goes to work in her garden, she leaves the infant in the arms of a nurse girl. When the baby has grown large enough to hold another baby, she becomes a nurse girl herself. There is no rest for these little workers, for they are also expected to go to the spring and bring back water in their little clay pots. As she gets older she brings more and more water at each trip, carrying it in larger pots until when she is twelve years old, she carries a pot containing about four gallons on each trip. When the family water pots are full, she must then go out and look for firewood; and when there is enough firewood for the evening meal, she must grind the grain into flour on the grinding stone that is kept in each hut. By the time she is twelve, she ceases to be a nurse girl and goes with her mother to dig in the gardens.

"At about this age, or a little earlier, she has her body beautified by some old women trained in the art. There are many different patterns which they use on the abdomens, such as diamonds, curved lines, and lines in the shape of the letter

103

S. The actual cutting is done by knives, thorns, and a special, stiff kind of grass. When the cuts are healed, the scars appear like black beads set in the skin. The decorations start from the navel and spread outwards. Their foreheads have lines from one temple to the other. Sometimes this is a single line, and frequently there are two parallel lines. The cheeks are decorated with three vertical cuts, the center cut being the longest, usually one half-inch long.

"When she is about fourteen she is sent to a girls' dormitory, where other girls her own age spend the night. Here, the young men come and make love to them. Special care is taken that the actual physical signs of virginity are not destroyed. But technical virginity is the only thing that is kept. Frequently, it is in these dormitories that the young men decide on their wives-to-be.

"As soon as the father of a girl learns that a boy has set his heart on his daughter, he goes to the market and other public gatherings and announces that his daughter is prepared for marriage, but the one offer he has is so small that he will never part with her for it, for his daughter isn't a 'gourd of dirty water to be thrown away for nothing.' The father invites proposals for his daughter in this way. Usually this action brings proposals from older men with several wives who can offer larger doweries than can the younger men. This sets up competition which pushes the price higher and higher. . . .

"Occasionally a kind-hearted father will not contend for more cattle than the boy who wants his daughter can pay. But most of the fathers are more interested in acquiring cattle than in their daughters' happiness. Many times girls are sold against their wills to old men because the young men they really love don't have the wealth of the older men. Sometimes the girls feel this injustice so keenly that they run away from their old husbands and refuse to consummate the marriage. Then the husbands appeal to the native court for help. The courts order the girls to be beaten with a *kiboko* and returned, but sometimes the girl will keep running away until she wears her father out and gets his consent to marry her true-love for a reduced dowry.

104

"More often than not, when a girl knows that she is being advertised, she will elope with the one she really wants to marry. Her father, then, is almost helpless in demanding a high price; for a girl who has lost her virginity has very little value in the eyes of prospective husbands."

Mother felt a cold chill in her heart as she considered the possibility that Haabwe would follow this last maneuver. She pointed out the value of chastity and told her she hoped she would be faithful to her Christian convictions.

"I know what you are saying is true," she replied, "but you will have to pray for me because I am only a girl and a beginning Christian, and my heart isn't very strong. I want you to pray that God will give me the strength to do the right thing."

Mother and Haabwe knelt together and prayed. When they got to their feet, Mother couldn't speak for a moment, for she visualized herself in the weeping black girl's place. She slipped an arm around Haabwe's slim waist and said, "Always remember that I am praying that you will do the right thing."

Shortly after Haabwe left, Jairo came to the door with the announcement that there had been a fight in one of the villages, that a little old man had almost been killed and was waiting for treatment at the hospital. Jairo insisted that the case was so critical that he could not take care of it himself, and so Mother dropped her work and hurried over.

The little old man, dressed in only a goatskin, was a sorry sight indeed. As thin as a banana plant, and inches shorter than Mother, he had been cut and stabbed from head to foot. He was trembling violently as he stood at the door, for he was mortally afraid of the hospital and the white man's medicines. The only reason he was there at all was because his son had forced him to come.

As mother cleansed his wounds she said, "How did you ever get into a fight like this?"

"Oh, Mama," he cried, dozens of deep wrinkles forming on his already deeply wrinkled face, "they are trying to steal my gardens."

Later, his son explained that the boundary between his garden and that of his neighbor was quite uncertain. Each one had dug a little on the other in order to compensate for what he considered a previous theft of land by the other. These invasions in the other's territory had daily increased from a few inches to several yards. Finally patience had run out on both sides, and a fight had taken place on the Z-shaped border.

One arm had been hacked clear to the muscle. There was a deep gash on the right cheek, and the man's head was knotted and swollen from the blows of a *knobkerry*. After his wounds had been cleansed and bandaged, Mother ordered him to bed in the hospital.

But this was too much for him. He began to weep and to point to his village out in the reserve. "I'm going to die," he sobbed, "and I want to go home and crawl into my hut and die in the same place where my old woman died."

"You're not going to die," replied Mother grimly. "As soon as you get into bed, I'm going to pray that God will heal you."

The little old man pled and wept like a child, but since his son also pled with him to stay, he finally consented. Mother prayed for him, and immediately he began to relax.

Late that night, not being able to sleep because of a toothache, Mother got up and went to the hospital to see how he was getting along. Like all the other patients, he preferred to have his face covered and his feet exposed. The worn red blanket was around his head and he was sound asleep. She silently prayed for him and then returned to the house. On the way back she noticed Jairo and Neva standing in the moonlight. They were a good distance apart, for they always behaved very properly. But his glowing face and her scowling countenance were a good indication that a romance was getting started. Mother was pleased, for she felt it was a good match.

Each morning the little old man was carried outside so that he could listen to the gospel sermon that was preached to the patients. And the preacher for the occasion never had a better listener. He followed every word, unconsciously forming them with his thick lips. But there was always a look of acute disappointment on his face. This puzzled everyone. Then one morning he motioned Mother to his side. "Mama," he said with deep emotion, "I would like to be a follower of Jesu Christo, but I can't."

"Why not?" interrupted Mother eagerly.

"Because I d-don't have any clothes. All I have is this goatskin."

As he finished, he burst into a fit of weeping.

"But you don't have to have clothes to be a Christian!" exclaimed Mother. "God doesn't look at our goatskins or our clothes. He looks at our hearts. All you need to do is to confess your sins to Jesus Christ and to believe that he died personally for *your sins*. When you do that, he'll fill your heart with love and happiness, and you'll love everyone—even the man who tried to kill you. You'll become a new person."

The next day the old man's face was radiant. "I'm new," he exulted. "I believe that Jesu Christo paid the price of my sins, and I'm new." He was so happy he almost jumped for joy.

Then, while Mother rejoiced with him, he said, "Now I want to be baptized."

He never mentioned clothes after that.

About a week after Haabwe's conversation with Mother, she was returning from the spring with a pot of water on her head when suddenly she was confronted by her father.

"I have received the dowry for you, and I have arranged for you to go and live with your new husband," he said, blocking her way on the path.

"But I don't want to marry him," replied Haabwe, greatly alarmed. "I want to help start the New Africa Mama is talking about. I am a Christian. Christians only have one wife."

"It doesn't matter to me what you think," replied Elijah coldly. "You are my property and seven fat cows are better than three thin ones. You will have to do what I say."

He then seized her by the wrist and led her over to his house. "You can put the water on the ground," he said, pointing to the pot on her head. "Your new husband will be here in a short time. Remember you are his property now. Your brother will use the cows he brought for you to buy a wife for himself. If you run away I'll have to return the cows. But that won't be the end of it, for if you run away, I will have you beaten until you'll swell up like a box."

As the old man who had paid for her approached through the surrounding banana trees to take her home, Haabwe prayed for wisdom. Biting her lip, she wrestled with her conscience. Sweat formed in the whites of her hands, and a cold feeling spread through her stomach. She knew that there were some women whose husbands had other wives and yet who allowed them to attend the church services and serve the Lord. Many of these husbands respected their Christian wives and did not force them to make beer or even raise tobacco.

Haabwe did not want to cause trouble, especially trouble that might hinder the missionaries. A wild thought that it might be best to submit presented itself, but as she watched the balding man striding eagerly toward her, she knew that she could not bear to live with him or to become the mother of his children. She also knew that her heart belonged to Oriedo.

There was a large wart with sprouting hairs on the right side of her buyer's enormous nose. And as he grinned suggestively at her, his crooked, yellow teeth stood out in his wide mouth like the carrion-filled teeth of a hyena. When he drew near, she felt like a helpless animal in a snare watching the trappers approach. She had an urge to run, to get away, but her strength was suddenly gone.

With a rush he grabbed her arm in his clawlike hands and said, "Come let us go to my village. I have already paid for you, and your father has agreed that you are mine."

But Haabwe did not budge. His alcohol-drenched breath made her turn her head, and as she did so the spell was broken, and she felt strength flow back into her limbs. "I won't live with you. I won't be your wife," she half-screamed, shrinking into herself.

The old man answered by digging his nails into her arm and

pulling her toward the path that led to his village. Haabwe responded by sitting on the ground.

A crowd of naked children gathered and watched the struggle, and older women stopped and smiled around the stems of their pipes. These women felt that Haabwe's struggles were all part of an act—an act that is a definite part of the tribe's marriage customs. They remembered how they struggled with their husbands, and the show they put on for the crowd. They also remembered how their husbands had had to send gifts to their parents before they would agree to cook, dig the gardens, grind the flour, carry the water, or physically perform the wife's part of the marriage.

With Haabwe, however, it was no show. She did all she could to get away, but the old man was too strong and experienced for her. As they passed through the banana trees she flung her arms around one in desperation, but her strength was insufficient to hold on.

Finding that it was useless to resist, that her dress was being ruined, and that she was already bruised and horribly mauled, she got to her feet and followed her captor with only token resistance.

There were, as friends from the old days had explained, some definite advantages in being the wife of a polygamist. "Don't you know that you'll be the new and favored wife?" asked a girl with whom she had shared a dormitory.

Yes, Haabwe knew that. She also knew that she would have very little work to do for the first two or three years of the marriage. During this time she would be treated like the favorite wife of a chief and would only receive an occasional beating. She would take her turn with the others in cooking the evening meal for her husband in her own, separate hut, but that would be about all. However, she also knew that it would not be long until she would have to start working from morning until dusk in order to raise more crops to buy more cows to enable her husband to replace her with another favorite wife. But the thought that twisted a dagger into her heart was that this marriage would almost eliminate her from helping to build the New Africa Mama talked about.

Soon, the old man's village was in sight. It stood on a little hill, and like most of the other clusters of huts, was surrounded with banana trees. The husband's hut was in the center of the open space. Its round, cone-shaped thatched roof had a discarded "shoe off the leg of a white man's car" thrown over the top. This was for decoration and to keep the grass in place. An early missionary from Sweden had shown them how to use a simple, wooden thatching tool to even up all the grass, from the peak of the roof down to the edges. But this old man scorned these advances of the foreigners, and so his hut was thatched in the old way: The heavy ends of the grass faced the bottom in parallel lines like a terraced garden.

The mud walls of his hut had been splashed with white clay in careless, uneven circles. A fire smouldered between the triangle of stones in the center of the hut. And a cracked, three-legged stool stood on the right of the door. This stool, carved from a log, was reserved for the husband who used it while he sunned himself, watched his wives work, and idled away his time by pulling out his straggling whiskers with the iron tweezers hanging from his thick, wire necklace.

The oldest wife, wearing her tiny bead skirt, was digging a garden a few paces away. As they stepped between the huts, Haabwe noticed that the woman increased the tempo of her work. She was obviously going to have a baby at any time, but she had to keep toiling away until the very last moment. Any pause for rest would bring a whistling *kiboko* down on her sweat-shining shoulders and increase her already large collection of scars. Of course when the baby came she could count on a three or four days' break in her toil. Thoughts of this provided the only gleam in her heart.

She was digging with an old-fashioned *jembe*. The heart-shaped blade on this hoe was attached by its long, metal tail to one side of a two-inch-thick tree fork. This tapered tail was secured to the wood with a coil of papyrus rope. Such inverted V *jembes* are not as efficient as the new type which

110

have a hole in the blade into which is fastened a long handle, and they are much harder to use. The new kind could be purchased at Luanda, but the husband did not want to spend an extra cent. His mind was geared to bringing new wives to do extra work to have more children in order to increase his wealth. He was constantly remembering that four hens would purchase one goat, four goats would purchase one cow, and from five to seven cows would purchase one woman.

As Haabwe glanced at the first wife, she could see the marks of her years of disappointments, beatings, and heartaches. Most of her children had died, and her husband was blaming her and had beaten her because of their deaths.

All at once, and quite unexpectedly, Haabwe had a surge of new energy. Like a trout on a line, she wrenched herself from the clutches of the old man, dodged through the banana trees and started down the twisting paths like a fawn just escaped from a trap.

But her flight, like the flight of other Bunyore girls in the same dilemma, ended in disaster. She was cornered by some of her father's friends and dragged over to his village. Elijah met her with a series of oaths and a *knobkerry*. This particular club would have gotten him into trouble had he carried it in Nakuru or Nairobi, for the knob was so big he could not place it in his mouth and thus pass the test established by the clever police.

"What do you mean by running off?" he demanded, as he sent her sprawling with a blow from his club. "Now, I'll have to return the cattle!"

Haabwe made a ball of herself on the ground, wrapped her arms around her head for protection and prayed for help.

Elijah kicked her in the ribs with his foot. "That will teach you to disobey me," he snarled. "I knew you would get into trouble if I let you work for the people who came out of the water. This is what I get for letting you spend your days in a square house!"

He kicked her again several times and then proceeded to beat her with the handle of his club. He longed to use the

111

knobbed end, but his cunning brain told him that it was foolish to damage property with certain cash value.

Having exhausted his strength, he called in the strongest man in the community to finish the job. This man used a *kiboko* and kept at it until her body was crisscrossed by dozens of livid cuts. With no other place for safety, Haabwe limped into the mission and presented herself at our door. Mother choked back tears of anger as she examined her swollen and bleeding limbs. Then she applied hot fomentations to reduce her pain.

"Mama," sobbed Haabwe, "I have no place to go. If I return to the dormitory or my village, my father will turn me over to that horrible old man again. W-would it be all right if I stayed here and slept on the floor of the kitchen?" Mother agreed to her request at once, and so Haabwe began to spend her nights in the kitchen by the side of the cast iron, wood-burning stove that had been shipped out from Kalamazoo.

The missionaries took turns with the native evangelists in speaking at the Kima church. The preacher for a certain occasion was generally determined by the one who felt he had a "message." This time Mother announced that she wanted to take her turn.

Filled to the brim with her concern over the plight of native women, she spoke with tears and deathlike sincerity to the congregation that jammed the little building to the doors. Jairo interpreted for her as she described the place women have in the community and church.

Stirred to her very depths, she poured out long strings of purple adjectives—adjectives that could not be interpreted into Olinyore because they did not exist. Jairo did his best to transfer her thoughts and emotions to the people, but this was exceedingly difficult because of the inadequate vocabulary.

Mother's sentence: "It is wrong, horribly wrong, dreadfully wrong, terribly wrong, and morally wrong to treat your wives like dumb, driven cattle," was interpreted. "It is very bad to treat your wives like cows." Jairo raised and lowered his voice and swung his arms as she did, and the audience listened,

112

spellbound. Jairo's version—and he did an excellent job—was like a dripping faucet in comparison to Mother's Niagara. But the people could see the wrath in her eyes, and the men who were in the habit of slapping their wives around, sat goggle-eyed. Telling them not to beat their wives was like telling them not to spit in public.

Unfortunately for Dad and me, Mother got so carried away with her defense of Obunyore women, she forgot that she was supposed to stop at noon. I sat and squirmed as the minute hand moved down to twelve thirty and then started up to one. The air in the building was tight, for it was a hot day and the tall, narrow windows were not completely opened. My head began to whirl.

Finally, I could endure it no longer. Pointing to my stomach so that Dad would understand, I got up from my seat on the platform and slipped out the side door. Back at home, I was joined by Dad at one fifteen.

"Where's Mother?" I asked, for I was hungry and the cook was getting impatient.

"Oh, she hasn't even gotten to the beginning of the end," said Dad with a chuckle. "If the men follow through on all that she's telling them, the women will be so spoiled they won't even cook breakfast!"

Mother made her grand entrance at two o'clock. "So you walked out on me," she exclaimed, her blue eye and brown eye curiously alight. "You should have stayed with me. Twenty-two people accepted Christ, and all of the men learned what I think of wife-beating."

Dad wasn't sure whether Mother was happier about the converts or about what she'd been able to tell the men in regard to the treatment of their wives. But he was delighted that it had turned out well, for he always rejoiced in Mother's success and bragged about it wherever he went.

Mother's three-hour sermon, however, had not used up her entire supply of righteous indignations. All afternoon and late into the night she continued to talk about the injustice inflicted

113

on native women, and the more she talked the more furious she became.

A couple came in the next day to be married, and since Dad had forgotten about them and had left, Mother agreed to perform the ceremony.

This pair, from an unusually distant village, were dressed in the latest wedding fashion. The groom wore a pair of horn-rimmed glasses without any lenses and four of his front teeth were encased in copper caps made from a discarded gasket. The bride had powdered her face with cornmeal, and her head and shins were polished to mirror brightness.

The bridesmaid was expecting her new baby in a few days. She had been chosen because it was thought she would help guarantee the bride's fertility. But Mother seemed to see none of these things. Her mind was still filled with Haabwe's ordeal.

Addressing the groom, she asked the usual questions printed in the ceremony. But after he had said, "*Ndio* [Yes]," she continued with some of her own.

"Do you promise you won't beat her?" she demanded.

The groom gulped at that one, and his eyes nearly filled the frames of his glasses. His Adam's apple jumped up and down his narrow throat like a pump handle at a dry well, but Mother refused to go on until he agreed.

Then she pursued her advantage by asking, "Do you promise to send her money when you are working up-country? And do you promise to remember that she is your wife and not a cow?"

The wife, also, had to make additional promises. Perhaps the most important of these was that she wouldn't run off and refuse to cook when her husband had company. After they had both agreed to all these questions, she pronounced them man and wife and prayed that they would have a happy home.

But Mother's sense of triumph didn't last, for as soon as the couple got out of the church the groom had to start dragging the bride after him. The girl wrenched away from him at the corner of the mission and threw a rock at him. But the rock missed by a wide margin, and she never managed to run really fast enough to get away.

114

14

Many Americans, reading in their church papers about missionaries with servants, are a little envious. "It must be wonderful," they murmur, "to have servants wait on you hand and foot." But if these critics were on the field a few months, they would gladly exchange local help for an electric washing machine and the other timesavers available in the civilized world.

For one thing, electrical appliances are usually more reliable. They don't go on strike, they don't experiment with one's toothbrush, and they don't steal.

One of Mother's friends returned unexpectedly from a hunting trip to find his wild-eyed cook in front of his mirror, scrubbing his yellowing teeth with his new American toothbrush. Tired of using the frayed end of a stick, the cook was having a great time with the new tool. As he pushed it back and forth in his cavernous mouth, he hummed the current marketplace hit to the rhythm of the brush. One of the verses went like this:

> *Cook the food of the white man*
> *And then eat some.*

> *Cook the food of the white man*
> *And then eat some.*

The tune was not worthy of an Irving Berlin, but the words were quite descriptive of the normal practice.

The white man stood with tightly clenched fists and watched as the native made eyes and faces at himself in the magic mirror. Still totally unaware of the Bwana's presence, he scrubbed his teeth with the same amazing vigor he used to beat the white of an egg with a butcher knife.

When the cook was fired, he felt he had been unjustly treated. As far as he was concerned, anyone was free to use his toothbrush, and he didn't see why the white man should not be equally generous.

Many Kenya servants I knew had an unusual concept of

stealing. If one happened to find some of your money, he might take it and hide it in *your* house. If you didn't miss it and several weeks went by without your mentioning the loss, he would take for granted that you didn't need it, and he would keep it. But if you made an inquiry, he would begin to hunt, and presently the money would turn up in the most unexpected place.

If his object was a raise in wages, he might wait until you had company and were all seated at the table. Then he would call you into the kitchen and with a gloomy countenance say, "I'm not eating enough shillings. I won't do any more work until I'm eating three or even two more shillings each month."

Many white women carry a large ring of keys. This is because they have to keep everything locked up. If the cook is to bake a cake, the necessary ingredients are measured out and the lock is snapped shut. I knew a settler who used to count his prunes. And once, when three of the shriveled things were missing, he grilled the cook until the conscience-stricken man confessed.

Our cook, Hezekiah, however, had none of these defects. He was a dedicated Christian and trusted elder.

But Mother was determined that every moment and every shilling count for the Lord. She reasoned that Hezekiah already knew how to cook, and that his wages could pay some boys to prepare the meals and thus help them earn their way through the mission school and learn a valuable trade at the same time. It seemed like a good move.

Accordingly, she dismissed Hezekiah and replaced him with Ebitanyi—the Marigole whose leg had been amputated because of an ulcer—and another teen-ager, Lesero. Both of them were attending school, and this assured their way financially. The boys made an effort to learn to satisfy the strange appetites of the people who had come out of the water, and Mother and Father ate the boiled chicken along with the pinfeathers without complaint. But I couldn't stand it. In despair, I fled to the villages and gorged on flying ants.

One of Ebitanyi's tricks in those days was to prepare such enormous omelets we could not possibly eat half of what he served. Then after breakfast he would invite his friends over and feed them as if he were the Aga Khan. Eggs were only three American cents a dozen at that time, but when I learned that he had used as many as forty eggs at once, I determined to do something about it. The very next morning, after my parents had left the table, I loaded the remaining eggs with red-hot chili peppers.

The kitchen party that followed was a very interesting one, and I took a keen delight in noticing the huge amounts of water that were consumed. But when I walked through the kitchen the better to enjoy my victory, I felt like a man facing a firing squad. Ebitanyi's face was as black as pitch. The sight of his friends with their pink tongues hanging out of their dark mouths is one I don't care to forget.

One morning it was announced that the British School Inspector would visit the mission. This man stood between the missionaries and the tax money the Government would allocate for mission schools. His recommendations went a long way toward producing needed grants. Because of this the missionaries took care to have well-laid plans to present to him for future projects.

Mother prepared her plans for her dreamed of Bunyore Girls' School with great care. Then she wrote down her various arguments for the vital need of female education. Next she planned an excellent dinner for the inspector, and had Haabwe and Neva bake some bread and cookies in order to prove that native women could learn the arts of domestic science. Ebitanyi and Lesero were assigned to buy a choice section of meat and were told that they should take extra pains with the food.

Confident that the inspector would be impressed, Mother announced to the students at the Boys' School that Bwana Inspector was coming, and that all of them should be extra clean. She also announced that no one should come without any clothes—especially pants.

When the crisis day arrived, Mother and Miss Baker who had just returned from furlough, led the smiling inspector from room to room and prayed that the students would make a good

117

impression. The first two classes recited very well and Mother's confidence soared. Then she led the way to her drawing class. Here she felt the group would ring the bell, for she had a flair for pictures and had personally done a number of successful oils. The only hazard was that the wrong student be chosen for an impromptu drawing.

Holding his khaki helmet with its brass insignia under his arm, the inspector carefully looked the class over. Then, pointing to Samwelli, said, "Draw a pocketknife on the blackboard."

Mother gulped, for although Samwelli was an excellent English student, he was mediocre at art. As he fumbled with the chalk, Mother prayed. The finished drawing looked more like a boomerang than a knife, and Mother bit her lip.

"Where was that knife made?" asked the inspector with a scowl.

"Please, Sir," returned Samwelli with a grin that revealed his unusually white teeth, "it was made in Germany!" The inspector laughed, and Mother gave a sigh of relief.

But her relief didn't last long, for in the next room she discovered one of her brightest students sitting proudly near the front attired in a pair of old-fashioned lady's drawers. The yellow garment was complete with several rows of lacy ruffles. Where he had gotten them was a question for the scholars. With amazing dexterity, Mother called the inspector's attention to something else in another room and a seeming catastrophe was miraculously avoided.

Having survived these hazards, she was quite confident as she led our guest down the brown murum road to the mission house that a wonderful meal would be awaiting them. She had decided that she wouldn't say a word about the proposed school until the sumptuous meal was over, but that once it was over she would use all her arguments to prove that such a school should be started at once.

She pointed the official to a comfortable chair and then went into the kitchen to tell Ebitanyi it was time to serve the food. But the kitchen was empty and the big black cooking stove was stone cold. Flabbergasted, she went outside to discover

118

Ebitanyi and Lesero beneath the spreading branches of our backyard wild olive tree—in the midst of a wrestling match.

"I thought I told you to get our dinner on time!" said Mother, her voice shrill with emotion. "Now hurry into the kitchen and get started!"

"But we don't have any firewood," protested Lesero as he handed Ebitanyi his crutch.

"Then cut some," she snapped, her brown eye and blue eye flashing fire.

"And what will we use for water?" asked Ebitanyi, taking a long hop toward the kitchen. "I sent Haabwe to get some a long time ago and she hasn't returned."

As he spoke, Mother saw Haabwe, the empty pot on her head, speaking in lingering whispers to Oriedo at the corner of the chicken house. On the verge of tears, Mother said, "Haabwe, I have a guest, and we have to have water. Hurry!" Then, with arms akimbo she returned to the kitchen and laid out the necessary things for the meal.

Fortunately, Dad rose to the occasion by taking the inspector around the mission and showing him his agricultural experiments. For a long time he had been trying to get the natives to plant their corn in rows instead of broadcasting it. In order to clinch his point, he had planted two fields of corn side by side. One field was planted in rows, and the other native fashion. But, unknown to Dad, the field planted in rows was over an old ash heap, and so his experiment worked in reverse, and the unconvinced natives became more determined than ever to follow the old ways. Dad had thought it was a good joke, and he and the inspector laughed about it.

The meal turned out to be a success. With great effort, because of Miss Baker's coaching on "talking shop" at the table, Mother refrained from speaking about the school she desired; but she could not keep from reminding everyone that the bread and cookies had been baked by native women.

As the inspector reached for one cooky after the other, her confidence mounted higher and higher. Indeed, it got so high that when she insisted that he have a fourth cup of tea, she tipped the pot too high and the lid fell off and smashed the cup.

"Maybe we had better go into the living room," suggested Dad, again stepping in and saving a situation.

The inspector listened carefully as she advanced her arguments for the need of a girls' school. But when she was through, he said, "Mrs. Ludwig, I think such a school is needed. But right now all of our available funds have been allocated. The best way for you to get a Government grant is to get your school going, even if you have to start in a very small way at first. When we see what is being done, are convinced the women can learn, we may be able to help, provided you can get the necessary support and personnel from your Board."

Mother was overjoyed in spite of all the ifs, whens, mays, and provideds candidly pointed out in the inspector's answer.

"We'll start the school right away," she said, her brown eye and blue eye bright with tears of happiness.

"But what will you use for a dormitory?"

"We'll put them in our kitchen. If they sleep on the floor and alternate their heads and feet, we can take care of a dozen!"

After the Sunday morning service, Mother had an unusual request. "John, let's go to Kisumu and see if we have a reply from the Missionary Board about the Girls' School."

"But the post office isn't open on Sunday, and petrol is three shillings a gallon."

"Oh, I'll get the postmaster to open up for us," said Mother, her lips in a grim line. "Besides, we've never done this before. We might have a letter from the Board, and we deserve a little recreation."

Father drove to the postmaster's house, but he refused to get out and go to the door. Mother had her way, though, and in a few moments the little English postmaster who had been a telegraph operator in World War I, was unlocking the door. Then he stood nearby, rocking on his feet and beaming as Mother went through the stack of envelopes looking for the long brown one that would be from the Board.

There wasn't any mail from the Board, but there was a notice that an auction would take place the following week near the Kisumu airport and that a lot of corrugated iron would be sold.

Suddenly Mother put her hand to her jaw. "My tooth is beginning to ache," she said. "Let's hurry home so that I can put some oil of cloves in it. If only there was a dentist nearby. . . ."

15

Tuesday was an important day at the Kima Mission, for it was at dusk on this day that the native runner brought the large canvas mailbag from Kisumu and deposited it on our living room floor.

Preparations for this event were always carefully made. Supper would be served early. And then almost ceremoniously, Dad would pump up the Coleman lantern, push the table back, and make a wide circle of chairs. Next, while suspense mounted, he would open the big lock with the key he kept on his private chain, and pour the mail out on the floor while we hungrily watched like greedy vultures hovering near a dying kongoni.

If several ships had arrived at Mombasa the week before, the mail would be heavy; and for a moment we would forget about malaria, jiggers, funeral drums, blackwater fever, and even the steady hiss of the lantern as we looked at the pile of six-week-old letters and papers before us.

Dad would go through the mail and hand each piece to the proper person while he remarked, "Now be sure and put the letter back in its own envelope when you're through with it." This was an admonition Mother seldom heeded. The mail—even if it was only the Bushnell paper—was always too interesting to remember such a minor detail.

After the mail had been read and the letters shared, Mother would say, "Let's shake the bag again. There might be another letter on the inside." There never was, but the bag always got a sound shaking. By this time the lantern would be growing dim and Dad would pump it up again. Then following a few more remarks we'd straighten the room, and after Dad had repeated, "Be sure each letter is in its proper envelope," we'd go to bed.

On this particular Tuesday Mother had eyes only for the long brown envelope that would be from the Missionary Board. It even had priority over the letters from her parents which were carefully laid to one side.

Suddenly Dad spotted the anticipated letter and handed it to Mother. Her face glowed as she ripped it open and settled down to absorb its contents. Then her face fell. The Board did not object to the school being started. But at that time there was no cash available, and the Secretary tactfully stated that he could promise none in the immediate future.

Mother was almost convulsed with grief as she saw her plans coming to an end even before she got started. "It's so unfair for Americans to have so much and the Africans so little," she said over and over again between sobs. Then I discovered a wide brown package beneath the second-class mail. It turned out to be a record, a gift from a friend in California. I wound up the newly arrived phonograph and soon a thrilling tenor voice was singing.

> *God is still on the throne,*
> *And He will remember His own;*
> *Though trials may press us*
> *And burdens distress us,*
> *He will never leave us alone;*
> *God is still on the throne, . . .*

As Mother listened, her tears dried and confidence came back into her heart. Then she reached for her Bible and after reading several favorite promises retired for the night. After that, whenever a setback came, she would say, "Charles, play the record." She never named it, but I always knew which one she meant.

After breakfast the next morning, Mother said, "We've got to have the Girls' School, and I have received definite assurance that God will provide the money. If the Government won't give us a grant and if the Missionary Board doesn't have the funds, we'll get it elsewhere. God owns the cattle on a thousand hills." As she spoke there was great confidence in her voice, and she ended up with her lips pursed in a grim line—the old sign of immovability.

She got pencil and paper and began to make drawings of a suitable dormitory. Finally, when she had one completed that satisfied her, Dad went over it and estimated that it would cost one thousand dollars to construct. But a thousand dollars at the time was the same as a million, an impossible sum to obtain.

Always thinking and praying about her problem, Mother knew that a solution would come. In time it did come, and in a much simpler way than she had previously imagined:

"At night when I would be alone with my thoughts I could see into millions of homes in the United States, and back in their closets and up in their attics I saw ragbags stuffed full and overflowing with pieces of cloth left over when garments had been made, the owners expecting to make something out of them sometime, but with the rush of a busy life year after year passing without any use being made of them. My soul burned within me. God gave me courage to write again to our Secretary.

"I made a little paper booklet, and drew a picture on the outside of a ragbag, bursting out with material. Then I planned little garments which could be made from used materials and bits of leftover cloth: baby blankets, underwear for the children, petticoats for the old heathen women, dresses for the young girls, and trousers for our naked herdboys, chest protectors for the pneumonia cases, and many other garments. I drew a picture of each and explained how to make them. Then I wrote a letter to accompany it begging that our people might have the contents of the ragbags of the church. I pleaded for Africa, that she might be granted even that privilege. I mailed the booklet and my letter together, hoping to get something for Africa even in this way.

"This time I was not disappointed. Our Secretary had lists typed from the booklet and sent to different groups in the Church. The lists were put in the hands of the women, and soon a large shipment of garments was received. When notice came from Mombasa of their arrival, I told some of the native women about them, and asked them to pray that God would help us to think of a plan whereby we might get some money to start the foundation of our building. It was suggested that we have a sale and that we charge a little more for each garment than is required to pay the customs at Mombasa and the freight to Kisumu, and regardless of how small it might be, we would give it to Mr. Ludwig to buy cement to start the foundation."

Dad, being a poor salesman, took a dim view of the proposed sale. As a young farmer he had taken a load of cucumbers into Bushnell to sell. But finding it next to impossible to go to the homes of strangers, he had very few buyers. Hating to return with a full load, he tossed them into the ditches as he progressed down the road. His pride was worth more than the cucumbers!

Mother, however, insisted, and Dad backed her to the hilt.

"We began planning for the sale. Pupils in the Boys' School made tickets showing the prices of the various types of garments, and the girls sewed the prices on the garments. The new floor in our printing shop had been recently laid, and we decided to make booths in it—a separate booth for each price. We advertised the sale far and near. Hundreds of people attended, each going away with a garment and an understanding that a tiny part which they paid would be put into the new building. After the freight was paid we had one hundred and twenty-five dollars for cement."

Tremendously encouraged, Mother decided that she would have an advanced sewing class in order to train teachers to help in the school after it was launched. For, although she planned to teach the required Government curriculum, she intended to emphasize home crafts. This was in order to raise the standard of living in the villages, and also to provide an opportunity for the women to get employment as domestic servants.

Most of the women made great progress with their sewing lessons. Almost at once they were doing fancywork that was as good as any being done in the Colony. Mother was very proud of this, for she felt certain that success in this field would draw attention to the necessity and possibility of female education. Moreover, her success with the previous sale was an indication that money could be earned by this means—money that could erect buildings for the Girls' School.

Soon she had the girls working an old treadle sewing machine, turning out dresses and shirts as fast as their nimble fingers could make them. They were very adept with the *esibia* (sewing machine) and could make it hum with the speed of a modern electric. Mother, with the encouraging news from America that many ragbags were on the way, invested heavily in cloth and soon had row upon row of white shirts and dresses all trimmed in red.

Then she received word that the Educational Department was sponsoring an educational show at Mumias and that she was requested to bring some exhibits. Cash prizes would be given, and better yet, the work of her girls would be seen by Government officials from all over the district.

Mother's joy and enthusiasm reached new heights. It was during this period that she developed the habit of working around the clock, and getting the girls to do the same. Patterns had to be made, letters had to be written, plans had to be discussed. Besides the burden of getting the Girls' School launched, she had the heavy responsibility of the maternity work and her teaching position in the Boys' School.

She became so busy and had so many things to supervise, her pocketbook fattened from an average of eight inches to about ten inches. Father's embarrassment increased with its size. Nevertheless, Mother insisted on taking it with her wherever she went. All his complaints were met with the standard pursed lips and emphatic, "Never mind."

Once, having worked all night for two nights in a row, she

said, "Girls, I'm so tired you'll have to carry me home." She meant this as a joke, but in a moment they surrounded her, and she was carried home shoulder high in spite of her shrill protests.

Returning from Kisumu after having purchased several bolts of *Americani* (a cheap white cloth), Dad said, "I sure hope you can sell all those things you're making. Money is getting short, and I wouldn't be surprised but what hard times are just ahead."

Father hadn't been reading the stock exchange reports, for none were available. But he had been noticing the one-eyed fish woman who brought fresh fish to the mission to sell every Friday afternoon. In the beginning she had demanded and received a shilling for every four fish. Then the price slipped to five for a shilling, and then six, and then seven. And that week Father had received eight.

He didn't like it and was deeply concerned.

"Never mind, John," said Mother. "We'll sell· all that we've made and the people will demand more."

Dad knew better than to press his argument any further, for if he did she would be certain to remind him of the cucumbers, an event he didn't wish to remember. Moreover, he had an abiding faith in her prayers.

At the hospital the girls whom Mother was training, knowing of her responsibilities, tried to help as much as possible. But on at least one occasion this nearly ended in disaster. Mother knew that a maternity case had come in, for she had seen the heathen men entering the mission with the bed on their shoulders. But word kept coming from the hospital that she was not needed.

Taking advantage of the time, she went to bed. But just as she closed her eyes, a native girl trooped in with a little velvety baby in each arm. Mother started to extend her congratulations. Then she noticed two thin lines of blood on the floor. A hurried examination showed that the cords had not been properly tied!

Her weeks crowded with work, Mother was extremely happy.

Then on a Saturday when she returned to the mission, she found that Haabwe had brought out all of her shoes and had carefully polished them. She had also placed fresh flowers in all of the vases and had picked a large bowl of Mother's favorite berries from the valley.

Puzzled, Mother went out to the kitchen. "Where is Haabwe?" she demanded.

Her question was met with silence. Then one of the girls quietly said, "She has eloped with Oriedo!"

Mother, shocked, disappointed, and at the same time keenly sorry for the girl, crept into her bedroom to pray and weep for her and the New Africa she longed to see.

16

Feeling that the exhibition in Mumias would get her foot in the door to female education, Mother worked on plans for the "show" with the passion a dictator might have for a personal coronation. She believed in the Africans, especially in "her girls," and was confident they would be foundation stones in the New Africa she dreamed about.

As she prepared for Mumias, she went from place to place praying that everything would be just right and that the Lord would help her students carry away at least their share of the prizes.

Later she reported, "When we arranged our exhibit we were very proud of it. After the judges had finished their work, we were surprised to learn that we had received prizes on almost everything we had brought. Our outschool writing got first prize; the sewing of Mariamu got first prize; and Neva's bread also took first prize. When we considered how many contestants there were in each group, we felt much repaid for our trouble."

Back at home, Mother rejoiced because of the prizes; but her main joy was that African girls had shown that they could learn and do fine work. And better still, the Government had become aware of what *her* girls could do. She felt certain that a substantial grant would be coming in the days ahead.

With this in mind she worked harder than ever in preparing for a huge sale that would provide the money for the first dormitory. From the time she got up in the morning until she went to bed at night—if she went to bed—her conversation was mostly about the Girls' School. At family prayers, she always prayed about the School, and quite frequently after we had all prayed, she would say, "And now, Lord, we want to continue a little longer. . . ." Then she would pray about some new problem concerning female education that had just occurred to her.

At the auction sale at the Kisumu airport, Dad bought a grotesque iron monstrosity that had been, I think, a part of a cotton gin. It was knocked down to him because he had impatiently named a figure merely to start the bidding. Unfortunately, there were no other bids, and so it was his. While we were loading it into the truck, I said, "Dad, what on earth will you do with it?"

"I'm sure I don't know," he replied with a chuckle. "But when your mother sees it she'll say, 'Oh, John, that's just what we need for the Girls' School.'" And that is precisely what happened.

The following week in Kisumu, Mother went from *dukah* to *dukah* buying bolts of material for the forthcoming sale. As she went up and down the streets, her pocketbook increased in size until it resembled a peddler's suitcase.

While she hurried here and there, arms akimbo, her bursting pocketbook swinging at her side, Dad prayed for additional grace and hoped that none of the white people from the other missions would see them.

Her purchases completed, we drove over to Mohammed Ali's *dukah* and ordered soda. When the glasses were placed on the table, Mother noticed they were powdered with a thin layer of dust. "Please wipe them off," she said. She said this, even though she knew they would be wiped with a shirttail.

As we were finishing our drink, Ali said, "I almost forgot to tell you, Mrs. Ludwig, that a friend of mine wants you to go over to his *dukah* and speak to his wife."

"What about?" asked Mother curiously, as he jotted down the address.

"She will tell you when you get there," replied Ali. "But be sure and do your best."

"I sent for you," said the slender woman in a gold-thread sari, "because I have heard that you believe in prayer and that God answers your prayer." She led Mother to a little mango tree in the center of the enclosure behind her husband's *dukah*, and pointed her to a chair.

"What do you want me to pray about?" asked Mother, sniffing at the heavy smell of garlic and chapati and trying to keep from staring at the gold ornament in the woman's nose.

"Please, Mrs. Ludwig," replied the lady graciously, her dark almond eyes filled with kindness and hope. "I want you to pray that God will send me a baby!"

The two of them sat together and talked over the problem. Mother gave her some practical medical advice, told her of Christ, and prayed that her wish might be granted. Ten months later the wish was granted, and as a token of her appreciation the thankful woman presented Mother with a set of teak bookends carved in the shape of an elephant. Mother placed the bookends in her pocketbook and kept them at home in the living room. Later, she presented them to me.

On the way back to the mission, the truck began to cough and wheeze. Then it grunted to a complete stop. Dad wedged some stones behind the rear wheels, for the clutch and brakes needed repairs, and lifted the side of the hood. Examination showed a clogged carburetor and fuel line.

Clever at improvisations, he figured out a way to limp back to the mission. But to do this he would have to have a pair of scissors, a nail file, a razor blade, a long piece of friction tape, and a paper clip. Unfortunately, he had none of these things, Kisumu was ten miles away, and the sky was boiling with dark rain clouds. Remembering the long, deep ruts in the road leading through Maseno, he became desperate. As a last chance, he mentioned his needs to Mother who was calmly sitting in the cab reading a letter from Bushnell. She responded by opening her pocketbook and within thirty seconds every item was produced.

While the truck crawled slowly toward the mission, Dad was silently glad that Mother had a pocketbook, even though it was big and fat and embarrassed him every time she carried it in public.

That evening Mother announced to Ebitanyi and Lesero that she was going to replace them in the kitchen with girls. Other work was provided for them, and their places were taken by Angilimi and Ndosio, sixteen-year-old daughters from heathen families of a nearby village.

17

Every morning streams of African women, large baskets of shelled corn on their heads, passed the mission on their way to Luanda. Here they went from one Indian to the next until they sold their grain for the best possible price. The coins received in payment were then placed on a sisal string and worn necklace-fashion.

Suddenly this was changed.

The women continued to carry heavy loads of corn to Luanda, but most of them returned with the same loads.

A week before the sale, Mother asked Mariamu what was happening. "The Indians have lowered the price of corn until the women won't accept what they offer," she replied, shrugging her shoulders and carefully avoiding Mother's eyes.

Praying that the price of corn would go up and that the women would be enabled to buy the garments she had been making and receiving from America, Mother got the building ready for the sale. But as she worked, she noticed the number of people returning from Luanda with unsold corn was increasing.

"You are wasting your time in trying to have a sale at this time," concluded Nicodemo, a native businessman who dealt in corn. "Every day the price goes down. A while back we got seven or even six shillings a bag (two hundred pounds), and now we are getting only three shillings a bag." He held up three fingers and shook them to emphasize his point.

When the mail sack was opened that night, Dad read a letter from the Missionary Board indicating that all allowances had been cut 20 percent. And along with this bad news there was a notice that several boxes of garments had arrived from the United States and an almost impossible sum was due for the freight from the coast.

"Oh, things will be better in a few weeks," said Mother, trying to sound cheerful.

"But we'll have to go and get those boxes right away," said Dad, "and I don't know where we'll get the money to get them released. I'm afraid this is the end of the Girls' School for a while." They became so interested in discussing the problems facing them, they forgot about the lantern on the table. The wick had not been trimmed, and so the flame kept growing on one side until the chimney was all smoked up.

Finally, Mother said, "Charles, play the record." I played it and immediately everyone felt better. Then Mother got up. "I'm going to bed and pray that God will show us what to do," she said. "He healed me when I was given up to die; he pushed down the walls of Jericho; he called us to Africa and provided the way. I know that this is his work and that he has a plan to supply our needs regardless of our allowances and what the Indians are paying for corn!" She finished with her lips pursed in a grim, straight line which we could all see in spite of the smoky lantern. They seemed to be underlining the promises.

That night as I quarreled with the malaria that had been nibbling away at me for several days, I could hear the sounds of the various powers that were at work in the heart of Africa. From a distant village to the north came the thump, thump, thump of funeral drums mingled with the shrill wailing of those who had lost a loved one or who had been hired to wail. Following the drums was the mournful sound of funeral horns that were blown because of the same death. Then a hyena howled in the Bunyore Hills.

A few minutes later I heard the Christians singing in a village that bordered Kima Mission. They were singing a favorite song about immortality to the haunting tune of "O Happy Day." Apparently someone had died and they were letting the people in other villages know that their friend had gone to be with the Lord "where there is no death."

While I was listening to the sorrowful and yet joyful Christians singing with the assurance that only converted Africans seem to achieve, I heard Mother praying. "Dear Lord," she said, speaking in the same tone of voice she would have used to speak across the room to me. "We are here because Thou did'st call us. Thou dost know the needs, every one of them. Thou dost own the cattle on a thousand hills. And, Lord, I believe that right now Thou art on Thy throne. We remember that Jesus said, 'Ask, and it shall be given you; seek, and ye shall find; knock, and it shall be opened unto you.' Now Lord I am seeking for a way to raise up a New Africa."

She was praying like this when I drifted off to sleep. How long I slept I do not know, for suddenly I was awakened by a jumbling noise at the door. As I stared through the darkness, I saw Mother approaching my bed with a candle in one hand and a glass of water in the other. She was dressed in her long, flannel nightgown, and her hair was done up in twin braids.

"My tooth is aching," she said, "and I got up to light the fire so that I could heat some water for the hot water bottle. Then I thought of you. You looked so white at the table. Here is some quinine."

I swallowed the drug and then listened as she went on to the kitchen to get the fire going for the water. Another hyena howled in the far distance, and then I went sound to sleep. When I awakened, the sun was shining through my window.

"Well, I know how we're going to get the money for the Girls' School," said Mother triumphantly as she squeezed some lemon on her papaya.

"How?" asked Dad, still as practical as ever.

"I'm going to trade the clothes to the natives for corn. Then I'll keep the corn until the price goes up—way up. When the price is about three times what it is now, we'll sell it and use the profit for our first dormitory. After that—"

"You should have been a Wall Street speculator!" interrupted Dad after he'd almost choked on his omelet. "Don't you know what you have said is ridiculous, impossible?"

"What's impossible about it?" asked Mother, her lips starting to form a line.

"Well, in the first place, where would you store it? We don't have a single crib on the whole mission," he said after he had gulped down his daily ten grains of quinine.

"You could put some of it in Charles's room," put in Rosalyn brightly.

"And if you did buy a lot of corn, how would you get rid of the weevils?" Dad continued, scowling at the taste of the quinine. "You ought to know that any corn that is kept over three months will be eaten by the weevils."

"Maybe we could get a medicine that would keep them out," suggested Mother.

"It can't be done," replied Dad emphatically. "The Murrays tried that up at Ingotse. They got the very best medicine that could be had in Nairobi, and paid a big price for it. It kept the weevils away for awhile, but it ruined the corn. Even the meat of the pig that ate the corn tasted like the medicine and had to be thrown out."

"But surely there is some way."

"I tell you, Twyla, it's impossible. I've ground corn in the hammer mill and I've seen the weevils come through alive. How they can survive the mill with the fine screens and the hammers whirling at 4,000 r.p.m. is hard to understand. But they do. The best thing for your plan is to forget it. An impossibility is an impossibility."

"What's impossible with man is very possible with God," replied Mother firmly as she gave the table a whack with her doubled fist. "This is God's work and he can take care of a few weevils and the price of corn!"

The response to the announcement that unshelled corn could be traded for clothes was very great. Soon the women crowded

133

into the misson with enormous baskets of corn on their heads. They had been requested to bring unshelled corn, for Mariamu had convinced Mother that it would resist the weevils better if it remained on the cob. Besides this, Mother knew the cobs could be used for fuel later on.

The corn was laid out on the ground in long, parallel rows in front of the laundry. It was my job to count the ears and write the number of them on a ticket. This ticket was then taken to the sale and exchanged for clothes. If the number was insufficient for a certain garment, the customer had to bring more corn.

Frequently a lot of tiny nubbins were poured out before me. When I insisted on placing several of them together in order to equal a regular-sized ear, the women protested. But when I refused to budge, they laughed, spat on the ground, and prophesied that I would grow up to be a rich businessman.

The corn, as Rosalyn had suggested, was stored in my room. But when it kept coming and more space was needed, I suggested that it be dumped in her room. This was done, and, I must admit, to my great satisfaction. Then we filled Mother and Dad's bedroom, the kitchen, and the living room. Next we moved out. But this we would have done anyway, for the Kramers had vacated the main mission house when they left for America. It was waiting for us to move in.

Surprisingly, one of the most popular items at the sale was a large selection of baby bonnets. Most of the mothers, however, did not buy them for their babies. They bought them for themselves. Indeed, it became quite a fashion, even though it was difficult, to tie the ribbons under their chins. Bonnets made from the tops of women's hose, with a dash of frilly lace thrown in, were the most popular.

They were frequently worn by stout women clothed in nothing else but skirts. Had these fashion plates appeared in this attire on Broadway, they probably would have snarled traffic for hours; but in Bunyore they were met with only admiring glances. Mother tried to show them that the bonnets were meant for the babies, but she had little success.

Nevertheless, many substantial garments were sold to the villagers, and the natives were very thankful for the generosity of the woman of the white man who made the sale possible by purchasing their nearly unsalable corn.

At the end of the week the clothes were all gone and the laundry was packed beyond the tops of the doors and windows with corn.

The only problem that remained was for the corn to triple in price, and for this to happen before the weevils had completely devoured it. From that day on, whenever we went to Kisumu, I was required to find out the latest price of corn from the Nyanza Oil Works and report the price to Mother.

Since I was in the corn business myself, this was no problem. I had developed a system of buying a two hundred pound bag of rock salt, going through the villages with my playmates, and trading a tablespoonful of salt for an ear of corn. My business was very good, for I always tripled my money. Having no overhead—the native boys worked for free—I felt I was a prosperous businessman. In time I hired an adult worker and began to pay cash for the corn.

Whenever the price of corn went up a few cents, Mother's confidence soared, and she would get out plans for the dormitory. But when the price sagged she had me play the record. One playing was enough to revive her spirits—except the day the weevils got in the corn. On that day, I had to play it a half dozen times.

18

Haabwe was close to death as she painfully turned half-closed eyes toward Mother from the bed on which she had been carried from the distant village.

Her entire body had been nicked by the witch doctor until there was not a square inch of flesh that had escaped his dirty, petal-shaped knife. He had then chewed a special grass until it was like masticated spinach, and had spat it all over her until she was splotched in green.

"Why did you let them do this?" demanded Mother, making a great effort to speak in a calm voice.

"I-I didn't w-want them to, Mama," she replied brokenly, muttering through unevenly swollen lips. "But my husband's relatives are heathen, and they wouldn't let me come to the mission. I begged and begged, but they refused. They said, 'The witch doctor has more power than the woman of the white man.'"

Mother had her carried to the hospital. But when she got there she found the building swarming with patients—many of them desperately ill. The bed she had in mind had been taken by a child that had fallen into the fire and was nearly dead. There was not a single spot where she could be placed. Mother thought of making room by sending a nearly well patient home, but her conscience wouldn't allow it. Then her brown eye and blue eye lighted up. "Take her back to our house," she ordered. "We'll block off the front hallway and keep her there."

While this was being done, she thought of the coldness and even the hostility of many Americans toward missions, and of their wealth even in depression years. She knew that many farmers would not keep their cows in the building she was forced to use for human beings. As she considered the unfairness of it all, her heart ached with a combination of pity, anger, and grief. "They have so much and we have so little," she kept repeating to herself while she took Haabwe's temperature and considered what to do. The thermometer indicated a temperature of 106.

After quoting some Scripture in Olinyore in order to increase Haabwe's faith, she implored the heavenly Father to have pity on the African girl who had suffered so much. Then she made her as comfortable as possible and had special broths prepared and taken to her from our own kitchen. Realizing that only a miracle could save her, she spent every possible moment by her side, even though this frequently meant having her lunch or tea in the hallway.

The instant Haabwe was strong enough to carry on a conversation, she beckoned to Mother and whispered, "Mama, I want you to forgive me for eloping. I know that I was a great disappointment to you, and that I have not helped build the New Africa you have talked about. But I didn't want to marry that old man. . . . I just didn't know what to do." She finished in a burst of tears.

Mother assured her that she was forgiven and urged that she only think of the future. Then as her strength increased, Haabwe related the things that had happened during her illness.

After the witch doctor had cut her and she didn't mend, he said, "An enemy has placed a broom in your stomach. This broom is being held within you by an evil spirit. If I am given a goat to sacrifice, I will make the spirit happy and he will release the broom and you will get well." The goat sacrifice was made. The witch doctor guzzled his share of the meat and spat out chewed-up pieces for the spirits, but she did not improve. This time he shook two gourds above his head and after mumbling magic words, solemnly declared, "The spirit holding the broom is very angry. This spirit belongs to the body of your dead uncle. We will dig up his body and burn it, and that will kill the spirit and you will get well."

The body was exhumed and burned according to directions. But even though the last bit of bone was reduced to ashes, her illness continued. It was then she persuaded Oriedo to allow her to come to the mission. And since he felt there was no hope for her recovery, he agreed.

Haabwe seemed to be winning the fight when suddenly she had a relapse and her fever soared. "Mama, I'm not going to live," she confided early one morning after refusing to eat. "I have prayed much about it. God has shown me I'm going to die." She paused for a tense moment and a shadow of thought crossed her pitted face. Then she took Mother's hand in hers and continued softly, "Mama, I didn't help build the New Africa with my life. But I would like to help build it with my death. I want to have a Christian funeral, and I want you to tell the people I don't want them to wail."

Mother promised, and then turned her face to keep Haabwe

from seeing her tears. A week later, as Haabwe had predicted, she died. Dad made a coffin out of pine boards and Mother lined it with *Americani*. Then she dressed the body in a favorite white dress, placed it in the coffin and arranged frangipani blossoms on top just as she had done for Henrietta Kramer.

The news of the death spread to the villages in minutes. Soon the mission was filled with relatives and the curious. The coffin was placed on our back porch. From here it would be taken to the grave that had been opened in Elijah's front yard. As the heathen stared sullenly at the body, they began to wail and shout obscenities directed at the missionaries.

"She died because she lived in a square house," shouted one old man as he stomped his foot and defiantly waved his beer-stick.

"Haabwe is dead. Haabwe is dead," wailed others. "Now, who will cook for Oriedo? Who will dig his gardens? Who will carry his water? Who will cook his *obusuma?* Who will bear his children?"

Soon a group of older women were swaying their bodies back and forth to the rhythm of the sentences that were being shouted about the deceased. Then others began to scream and shake their palms in front of their mouths, thus producing a hyena-like sound.

Mother and Dad went into the house to get something, and while they were gone a young man leaped onto the porch, snatched the body out of the coffin, and ran away with it. Elijah, however, rallied to the cause and ordered it returned. "Haabwe said that she wanted a Christian funeral," he announced, "and being her father, I say that she will have one!"

The body was returned, wedged again into the coffin, and the funeral services proceeded with a minimum of wailing.

That night the heathen blew their funeral horns and beat their funeral drums while the Christians sang about immortality. It was a decided contrast.

"John, we must build that first dormitory," said Mother as she poured a third cup of tea. "We just can't go on like this. Haabwe died because of ignorance. If only she had come in

138

when she first became ill. . . . These native women must learn to take care of themselves and their children. Teaching the men is only half the job."

"I agree the dormitory should be built," replied Dad. "But what will you do for money? Are you willing to sell the corn?"

"No, I'm not willing to sell the corn until the price goes up. But maybe we could get some native workmen to lay the brick and let us pay them after we've sold the corn. I know I can get some women to work for nothing."

"But you'll have to have some cash right now to buy cement and nails and other things, and besides I am not sure the natives would be willing to wait for their money. They have to pay taxes when they're due."

"Well, we have the one hundred and twenty-five dollars we earned from the first sale."

"That's a good start, but it's not enough," said Dad reaching for the quinine bottle.

"But, John, we have to have the building. We simply have to have it. After we get the school going, the Government will give us a grant. I just know they will."

Suddenly her eyes lit up with an unusual, determined flame. "I know where I'm going to get some money and get it right away," she said, thumping the table with her fist. "I've been saving some money so that we could go to Kampala and get my tooth pulled. John, I can't spend that money for myself when you're here to pull it!"

"But, Twyla, I can't give you an anesthetic. It's been decayed for a long time and will probably break. I'm afraid it would hurt like everything," he exclaimed, visibly shaken.

"It will hurt worse if I don't get the dormitory started," she replied coldly, her lips in a grim, firm line. "Charles, go and call Miss Baker. I'll have her hold my hand while Dad does the pulling." Miss Baker held her hand on the front porch by the side of the lime tree, and Dad pulled the tooth. Fortunately, it came out in one piece.

A week later, when Mother learned that M. A. Baker was coming up from South Africa to visit his daughter, Mabel, and

139

the mission he had founded, her joy reached a new pitch, and the record was able to rest. I took advantage of this, to the delight of everyone but Mother, by playing again and again "The Wreck of Old Ninety-seven."

She and the staff decided that Mr. Baker would be the ideal one to lay the cornerstone of the new building. The women whom she approached for donated labor agreed at once. Phoebe said, "I know the school is needed, and I know the good it will do in Bunyore and in the villages where the girls will go during vacation time and after they have finished and are married. I can't lay brick, but I can carry them and I can pud mud. These two feet of mine are as tough and strong as any in all Bunyore!"

From the beginning, Mother had known it would be easy to find helpers and brick-carriers. Getting skilled masons to work without the promise of immediate cash would be the hard part. She went to Dad with the problem.

"Why don't you get Rubeni?" he replied at once. "He's an excellent brick man and a thorough Christian."

Mother knew all about Rubeni, for Mrs. Kramer and others had told her of his remarkable conversion and life. In his pre-Christian days his name was Esirengi (Leg). At that time he was in great demand as a dancer, for he had perfect rhythm and could twitch better than anyone in the area. He was also famous for the amount of beer he consumed.

After a funeral dance he had gone searching for a beer party and accidentally found himself in a church service instead. The sermon and the singing were to the point, and to the astonishment of all his friends, he decided for Christ. His conversion was as definite as that of Saul of Tarsus. On his way home he met and convinced his mother that she should become a Christian. Then he started a church under a tree. The congregation grew until a mud-wattle building had to be constructed. But soon this was overflowing. Then he got people to gather stone and using his skill as a mason erected one of the finest buildings in Bunyore. Later, feeling that he did not have enough education to tend the flock properly, he helped finance a young man's way through school and resigned in his favor.

When Mother placed her proposition before him, a wide smile crossed his light, pox-scarred face. "Mama, I'll be glad to help and even if you can never pay me, it will be all right. Jesu Christo has done so much for me, I can never thank him enough!"

19

A Czech businessman, Francis Paul, who later married my sister Rosalyn, prepared the foundation for the first dormitory and got it ready for the laying of the cornerstone. Mother stood and watched during every spare moment, her heart nearly bursting with pride and satisfaction. She felt that each stone, each drop of cement, was a contribution to the New Africa.

The day before the ceremony, Mr. Baker came over to our house for dinner. But once again the elaborately planned meal, designed to show the prowess of Mother's girls in baking, nearly ended in disaster. This time the trouble was that an insane man had wandered onto the mission. Whenever one of the girls started for the woodpile, he would charge after her, his wild, smoke-discolored eyes gleaming. Completely naked, his long sharp points of woolly hair loaded with feathers and string, he was a terrifying sight.

But when Mother saw him and realized what might happen to Indosio's biscuits, she suddenly lost all fear. Grabbing a broom, she scrambled off the porch and started after him shouting, *"Tsia! Tsia!"*

The man fled as if he had been charged by a lion, and the girls shook with laughter. "Now isn't the time to laugh," chided Mother, fixing them with her brown eye and blue eye. "Now is the time to get that stove hot and make the best biscuits you've ever made!"

Mr. Baker, who at one time had employed and befriended Mohandas K. Ghandi, was in his seventies. His straight white hair was neatly combed and parted on the left. A Christian

141

worker since his conversion at seventeen, he was full of exciting stories about his work for the Lord. At the time of his first wife's death he had set aside $7,500.00 to be used for evangelistic work among the various African tribes.

He told how Robert Wilson, who had been in charge of his work at the New Comet Mine, had read an article in a magazine which had inspired him to go up north to Kenya. He had supported Wilson financially, and two years later had sent a native convert, John Bila, to help him. Bila worked at Kima for three years and then suddenly passed away and was buried on the mission.

"When I brought my daughter to Kima in 1914," he said, after taking another biscuit, "there was a group of candidates for baptism—about fourteen, I think. I was amazed to learn how many had been converted through Bila's ministry. He was a great man of God. One of the most devoted men I've ever seen."

"We are thankful for the stones you laid for the foundations of a New Africa," said Mother, after listening politely to a number of remarkable anecdotes about the early days. "But you have arrived here just as we are entering into a new phase of the work." She then told him about her dream of establishing Christian homes where the children would be raised in cleanliness and decency.

"We have decided that you are the one to lay the cornerstone for the first building in the Bunyore Girls' School," she said hopefully.

"I am all for educating the women," he replied, his eyebrows creeping together, "but we must never confuse Westernization with Christianity. And I'm afraid that is what a lot of missionaries are doing."

Mother agreed with him completely on this point, and then she got started off on the blessings the girls could be in their various villages. She concluded by pointing out that the biscuits and bread had been baked by native girls, and that they were just beginning to learn.

Mr. Baker showed his enthusiasm for the work by writing out

142

and placing the following inscription in the cornerstone at the ceremony: "That our sons may be as plants grown up in their youth; that our daughters may be as cornerstones, polished after the similitude of a palace" (Ps. 144:12).

A long line of women carried brick from the kiln in the valley to the building site, and Phoebe proceeded to pud mud for mortar. As she worked she sang "Standing on the Promises" and kept time to the music with her big feet. When questioned what she was doing, she replied, "I am helping lay a stone in the foundation of the New Africa Mama has been talking about."

Rubeni and others laid the brick, and Mother's plan began to grow. She visualized a dozen dormitories, a domestic science building, a staff of white workers, students from a dozen tribes, and a Christian testimony that would stir the whole area. This dream was given great encouragement by Mr. Baker. The native churches, wishing to show their appreciation to the one who had made it possible for them to hear about Jesus Christ, made up a purse for him of nearly one thousand shillings. He, in turn, turned it over to the mission, stipulating that it should be used to build a house for the hospital attendant.

At the completion of the dormitory which was named Rosalyn House a meeting of the Church Council was called. After the men had inspected the building, speeches were made, and Mother spoke of her dreams. Then Daudi Otieno got to his feet, "I believe in the success of this school," he said, "because Missi Ludwig-i is a teacher like a European pot. Some teachers are like our pots, when they have corrected a pupil they just keep on boiling and boiling. Even after the fire is taken away, they boil on and on. When you take a European pot off the fire it stops boiling immediately. I have known Missi Ludwig-i four years now, and I have observed that when she corrects a pupil she never says another word. She stops boiling."

The Church Council was instructed to select twelve of the best girls in Bunyore to make up the student body. The tuition was set at fifteen shillings a year. Since common labor only earned six shillings a month, this was a stiff price. But Mother felt that they would appreciate their education if they paid for it.

The first day the girls occupied Rosalyn House was one of the three or four brightest days in Mother's life, and she wrote about it in her book, *Polished Pillars*:

"That night it was home sweet home in the new building. A warm fire was blazing in the fireplace, lighting the whole room enough so that Margret read out of the *Zaburi* a psalm for the evening worship. Then we knelt together and prayed that God would bless our school, and Rosalyn, who was then in America. It seemed that God let down His approval on us, while we were upon our knees. The girls have never forgotten the occasion and often refer to it.

"The next day we started fixing up the dormitory during our handwork period. The walls were not yet decorated and we did not have any money to spend. On inquiry, I learned from Mariamu where a bank of white clay could be found. Very early on Saturday morning six jolly adventurous girls started out from Kima in search of *obutoyi obulafu* (white clay). They went by the way of Ebusiratesi, and then on to Ebudongoi. It was quite dark when they returned, drops of *obujessi* (sweat) falling from their faces. All we could see at first was rows of white teeth, as they appeared out of the darkness. They had enjoyed the trip, and had also spread the *oluyali* (fame) of the school.

"One evening when I came into the sitting room to have worship with them, I had just opened the door when they began to sing a song they had composed which mentioned all of the school and dormitory equipment. The chorus to this remarkable song was, '*Embuo* [thank you], Mrs. Ludwig-i, *embuo.*' It was a song typical of the Negro people, with one leading in the verse and all joining in the chorus.

"I clapped so hard they sang it several times for me."

Mother insisted that the school be practical, and that it further the work of Christ. At the end of each vacation period the girls would gather in the assembly room and tell what they had done in the villages to help bring about the New Africa.

144

Top: Kenya Christians built this great church at Kima. Bottom: Mr. Ludwig is pictured baptizing converts in Kenya. They came as many as five hundred at a time after each had completed a Bible class.

Top: Some of Mrs. Ludwig's domestic science pupils. She thought this training was a key to building a "New Africa." Lower left: "Mama" with a few
of the nearly one thousand children she delivered. Lower right: A modern
Dr. David Livingston examines a little boy who fell into a fire.

At one of these sessions, Matroba stood and said, "I helped my mother get well by washing and dressing her ulcer each day. Now she can walk. I washed her old dress and made her a new one out of some material my father brought back from Nairobi. I planted a garden of *wimbe* in *rows* even though the people laughed at me. I carried all the water during my month's stay at home, and I cooked the meals. My father likes the new way we have of making *obusuma* by cooking it longer."

After everyone had clapped, one of the older girls, Khasante, got up. "I tried to teach our people at home that agriculture is not drudgery, but an honor to our women. I taught my mother and six other women to plant *wimbe, mutama,* corn, and potatoes in rows in order to make it easier to cultivate. I helped five women dig *humus* pits and taught them how they could produce *humus* to build up their soil. I helped dig a ditch around a hill and planted *olusi* [a heavy, cane-like plant] to prevent soil erosion."

Then it was Omukhasia's turn. "I helped my mother to wash," she began. "I dug some of our *emihoga* [casava] and used it to make starch for our clothes. I borrowed a charcoal iron from the Jeanes' teacher and ironed my mother's dress, and I wish you could have seen it. I carried wood, dug the garden, and brought water from the spring."

There was a lot of clapping when she was finished even though she had not done as much as some of the others. But everyone knew she came from a heathen home. Some of the other girls told how they had helped in the Sunday schools and how they had told their friends about Christ and what he had done for them. Mother was delighted.

But still no money was coming through from the Government, and funds were extremely short. Something had to be done about it at once. She was convinced that the school, even though it was very small, was fulfilling a need and that the Government would help if they only knew what was being done. And so she arranged an exhibition and invited neighboring missionaries and Government officials.

The School Inspector was impressed and mailed an excellent report. Miraculously, the Educational Department had one hundred and twenty-five dollars left over from the previous year. This they sent to Mother, and she invested it in some beds for Rosalyn House.

"When the twelve lovely iron beds came, we made corn-husk mattresses, taking a great deal of pains to make them nice. We did not have any money to spend for heavy cord to tie them; so several of the girls were detailed to the sisal patch near the Boma to bring back a few loads of the sword-shaped leaves. These leaves were beaten on a boulder until the green pulp had been smashed away, and then the girls rolled the fibers together on their knees and thus produced strong white cord. Next we cut circles from the scraps of blue cloth which the women from the United States had sent us from their rag-bags, and placed one circle on one side of the mattress and the other on the other side, and with a big needle—the only thing we had to buy—we sewed them together with sisal cord. The girls were proud of their mattresses, for they looked quite like those in the Kisumu stores.

"Then a box came from America laden with just the treasures we needed: sheets from unbleached muslin for the single beds; pillowcases from flour sacks; quilts pieced out of scraps; comforters from old woolen coats lined with outing flannel; pencils, chalk, erasers, writing tablets, and other school materials. We had enough such supplies to last us for a year."

Facing Dad across a pot of *Simba Chai* after the breakfast dishes had been removed, Mother was in an expansive mood and said, "Now we've got to think of the next dormitory because a lot of new girls have already started to apply. I think I'll call it Gladys House in honor of Gladys Kramer."

"Before we even think of another dormitory," put in Dad, pouring the tea, for Mother was so excited he was afraid she would break another lid, "we'd better pay for the one we've built. The flag is going to be raised at the Boma pretty soon, and Rubeni and others will want their money for taxes."

"But I can't sell the corn," interrupted Mother. "The price

hasn't gone up, and I absolutely refuse to sell unless we triple our money!"

"Maybe this will change your mind and bring you down to earth," said Dad, pulling an ear of corn from his pocket. A tiny, needle-size hole had been bored into each grain, and when he tapped it on the table a fine, dark flour sifted out.

Mother held the ear up to the light and carefully examined it. "What is the price today?" she asked, finally.

"Last week it was three shillings a bag."

"Then we're going to keep it, weevil or no weevil. That corn has to bring us enough profit to pay all our bills!"

"But if it gets any worse the Government may throw it in the lake. And besides, we've got to pay the men."

"Do you suppose the Church Council would give us some money from the Christmas offering?" asked Mother, changing the subject and pushing the weevily cob toward Dad. "They thought enough of Bwana Baker to give him some money, and they just might think enough of the Girls' School to give us some money."

Before Dad could venture an opinion, there was a loud series of knocks at the door and a voice shouted, "*Hodi* [May I come in]?"

Mother jerked the door open to find herself facing Jonah through the screen, and as she stared into his wild, bloodshot eyes, a cold terror gripped her heart. Years before he had cooked for Richardson. At that time he was an enthusiastic Christian and once, after an impressive meeting, he said, "Bwana, I want you to teach me to be such a good cook that when I get to heaven I'll be able to cook for God." But since then, native gossip had accused him of being an *omulosi* (a kind of witch specializing in creeping up on people at night and splitting their heads with a *knobkerrie*). Mother had personally given medical attention to a number of girls whose skulls had been cracked by some mysterious person, and so as she watched him she slipped the screen hook in place.

"Mama," he began, as he nervously rubbed the greasy handle of his huge *knobkerrie*, "my wife, Salomi, has been in labor all night. But nothing has happened. I have taken her to the hospital-i, and I want you to go over and help. If you don't help and pray to God, she will die!" While he spoke, his tightly drawn skin darkened until it was as black as a cooking pot.

Mother offered a silent prayer and then boldly stepped outside. I held my breath as I watched them heading toward the hospital together, for I was convinced that he *was* an *omulosi*. I was convinced because when I was only nine years of age, I had called him an *omulosi* to his face, and he had threatened to kill me. And that night, while my parents were at Ogada, he had come to the house with his *knobkerrie* to get me. Fortunately, however, the Kramer dog, Princess, had chased him away, and I was able to emerge from under the bed shaken, but alive.

Now I regretted that I hadn't related this history to Mother.

20

When Mother tried to examine Salomi to determine the difficulty, she screamed and pushed her hands away. Neva and two other girls came to help, but in spite of their coaxing, she would not be touched. Since it was time for the Girls' School to open, and since Mother was convinced it would be a most difficult forceps delivery, she left Salomi with the girls while she got the classes going.

But on returning with her instruments, she saw that Salomi had vanished. Knowing she would certainly die without medical help, Mother sent a couple of girls to look for her. In Mother's words, "After some time they returned saying she was hidden in the banana trees south of the hospital and refused to come with them. I then went with the girls and coaxed and pleaded with her for a long time. Finally, she decided to return with us, although she still refused to allow me to make an examination.

"But toward evening, I finally persuaded her to let me put her to sleep so that I could know what to do. I found that the child was dead and was getting ready to deliver it, when Jonah pushed in. 'I refuse for you to touch her unless you have an *omudoctari* to help you!' he announced, his black skin clinging even closer to his skull.

"Since three young men, who had insisted on being circumcised in the absence of the doctor, had died from an overdose of ether in a nearby hospital and a great fuss had been made about it by the Medical Department, I decided to let her wake up and summon a doctor. Mr. Ludwig was away at the time, and so I asked James Murray to go to Maseno for their doctor.

"Mr. Murray went over on a bicycle and about two hours later a car drove up. I hoped that it was a doctor, but instead it was Archdeacon Owen. He explained that their medical man was away, and that he would do what he could to help. In earlier days he had done a lot of maternity work, for he, like many others, had studied obstetrics in his preparation for missionary work. Fortunately he brought a nurse.

"After Salomi had been put to sleep again we worked for several hours, but without result. Her pulse began to get thready, and I explained this to the Archdeacon, and he graciously submitted to my fears and suggested that I let the case rest overnight. I thanked him with all my heart for coming and doing his best. This experience always made me have a fellow missionary feeling for the Archdeacon, although our paths of service were in very different channels after that night.

"I let Salomi wake up and put her to bed, then sent for her sister to watch her through the night. I put a hot water bottle to her feet and wrapped her in blankets. It was midnight when I got to bed.

"But just as I was falling asleep, I heard a noise on the veranda. Then a shrill voice called out, 'Missi Ludwig-i, come quickly and examine me. Please! Please!'

"'All right, Salomi, go quickly and get on the table and I'll be right over,' I promised.

"When I got there, however, she rebelled again. One of the girls from the school was present and she said out loud, 'All right, Mama, you just go back to bed. Salomi doesn't *really* want any help.' We both went outside and made noises on the ground as if we were leaving, but we stayed. Pretty soon I heard her get down off the table. I thought I had better look in, and to my utter astonishment I saw her lift my basin of strong antiseptic solution to her mouth.

" 'Don't drink it, or you'll die!' I screamed, rushing toward her.

"At daylight two elders of the church came over to hear the news. Learning what had happened, one of them laughed: 'So you still have work to do.' I replied, 'Please get the Christians to pray that I will have success. Without God's power I can do nothing.' "

By early afternoon the baby was delivered. It had been dead for quite a while and Mother estimated that it weighed at least twelve to fourteen pounds. But this experience got her to writing and praying that a delivery room and a doctor would be supplied.

Later, she wrote, "In the latter part of 1934 I had a visit from Dr. Connelly, the medical officer in our district. I began telling him of our work in this department, and he said he had been investigating it at the Boma and had found the reports to be true. He told me that the Government wanted to give us a maternity ward and a delivery room in connection with our Girls' School. Later, the money was paid to Mr. Ludwig and the building was erected. It was dedicated July 4, 1935."

After the baby had been delivered, Mother went down to the laundry to have a look at the corn. It was even worse than she had imagined. The moment she opened the door, she could hear the faint hum of the weevils at work. They sounded like a distant airplane.

"What are we going to do with the corn?" she demanded, as she faced Mariamu. "If these weevils continue, we'll have to throw it all out and we won't be able to pay our bills."

"There is only one answer, Mama," replied the sewing teacher, a deep wrinkle crossing the smallpox vaccination on her forehead. "We will have to spread all the corn out on the foot-

152

ball ground and let the sun shine on it. This will help. I know, for I have done it before."

"But will it take care of it?"

"Perhaps."

After an announcement in the Kima church, dozens of women came to move the corn. But since the laundry was at the other end of the mission, this was a very difficult job. And to make matters even worse, we were then in the rainy season. This meant that the corn had to be spread out in the morning and then carried back in the afternoon before the four o'clock rains.

The corn was moved back and forth in this fashion three times a month. Dad watched and listened as the women worked and sang, but he knew they would never get rid of the weevils. They were just too incorrigible to be discouraged by a little sun. He was afraid that all of it inevitably would be dumped.

"You'd better plan on selling the corn," he said one night after the mailbag had failed to produce a shilling or even the promise of a shilling. "The way the weevils are tearing into it, it won't last a month."

"But the price hasn't gone up," said Mother from behind the Bushnell paper.

"It's better to get three shillings a bag than nothing."

"Who said we're going to get three shillings a bag?" replied Mother with just an edge of sarcasm in her voice. "I'm going to get my price, or nothing. I have prayed about it, and I have been assured that this is God's work and that he will take care of it and see that all the bills are paid."

Realizing that her greatest potential supply of money for the school was from the Government, Mother slaved at producing quality and displaying the girls' work whenever she had an opportunity. Her demand for quality reached almost unbelievable proportions. The paths around the buildings had to be constantly swept; the white edges of the girls' feet had to be sparkling white, and the dead skin on their heels had always to be rubbed off; the flowers lining the paths had to be trimmed and weeded; the stones outlining the paths had to be whitewashed; the buildings had to be spotless; and the registers had to be kept up to date and on easy display.

Moreover, the girls had to learn and produce good work. Since one of the avowed purposes of the school was to teach domestic science so that the girls could be better wives and mothers and get jobs, Mother labored hard to teach them these things.

No one knew when the Inspector of Schools would show up in order to write a report—a report that might produce or cancel a grant.

The Bunyore Girls' School was in peril at all times!

But in order to have breathtaking displays and to produce enough garments and fancywork to earn an income for the school, Mother had to draw most of the patterns herself. She frequently worked all night at this, for they had to be just right. People marveled at how she could work night and day, day after day. But to her it was no problem. She had a vision of what Christ could do for Africa, was convinced that she had been called to this work, and believed that the One who had called her would supply the energy. Besides, she was constantly prodded by the early morning funeral drums and horns.

Also, Mother had developed a way of leaning on the Lord while she worked. In a birthday letter to me, she mentioned this source of strength: "Should I never see you again in this world—if it is possible from the Heavenly Country to send you special help—I will fling you 'special anointing' like manna was given the Israelites, to go on with your work.

"Please believe me when I say that the only secret is staying very near to the Father through constant communion with Him. *This can be done even as you continue your work with your hands or brain, when you have learned the secret of doing it.*"

Another missionary relates that once at 3:00 A.M. when she went to summon Mother to an emergency at the hospital, she found her busy drawing patterns for the Girls' School. "You shouldn't be working at this time of night," she said.

"Oh, I'm not working," replied Mother, offering her a cup of

154

tea. "I'm relaxing. When I get through with these towel patterns, I'll start on my mail. I have about thirty letters to write."

But all of this work, anxiety, and planning meant that sometimes a whole week went by during which I never had a conversation with Mother. Fortunately, I had become an avid reader; and even though a period of two years went by during which I never saw a white face from outside the mission staff, I managed to keep reasonably happy by going on imaginary trips with various authors.

I used to hang a lantern over the post of my bed and read until late. More often than not, someone would push into my room and take the lantern just as I was getting interested. "The lantern in the hospital has a leak in it, and a baby has just come in that fell into the fire," was a typical excuse. Or, again, I would be told, "The lantern at the Girls' School has been stolen, and we have to take yours so we can have evening devotions."

I seethed inside over these things, and one day I exploded. "All I hear is Girls' School, Girls' School, Girls' School," I shouted, losing complete control of myself. "When we pray, we pray for the Girls' School. When we get the mail, it is to see if there is a letter about the Girls' School. When we eat, the conversation is about the Girls' School. When we go to Kisumu, we have to buy something for the Girls' School. And when I'm not hearing about the Girls' School I'm hearing about Mariamu, Leyha, and Margret.

"I'll tell you I'm getting fed up. I wish a bolt of lightning would come and smash the school. If I were to break my leg you'd say, 'It's too bad.' But if Mariamu stubbed her toe, you'd turn heaven and hell to fix it.

"Why, oh why, do I have to live in this horrible land? Why couldn't I be in America with other boys where there are exciting things to do?"

After I had run down, Mother said, "Many boys in America would give their eyes if they could exchange places with you. This is a wonderful country. Last month you got to go out with Dad on Lake Victoria and shoot a hippo—"

"What's interesting about shooting a hippo?" I asked, interrupting her. "I'd a million times rather be able to go to a store and get a hot dog with real catsup on it. Last night I was reading about Indians. But do I get to see Indians?"

"Kisumu is full of them," said Dad with a chuckle.

"Yes, but those are Indians from India. They're not *real* Indians. I'll tell you something. I'd rather be dead than live here. I'm always hearing Mother tell how she went to my crib and consecrated for me to go to Africa. Well, I wish she'd asked me about it.

"Other white boys get to go to school and play ball with each other, but I have to take my school through the mail!"

By this time I figured I'd earned a thrashing, and that anything else I'd say would not merit extra punishment, and so I stood up and fairly shouted, "I wish this mission, the Girls' School, and the hospital were all in ——!" I mentioned a place frequently referred to by theologians.

But instead of Mother reaching for a stick, she looked at me with a faraway look, and I thought I saw just the hint of mist over her brown eye and blue eye. Then she said, "Charles, what would you like to have for Christmas?"

This unexpected reaction stunned me for a moment. I could hardly believe my ears. When I regained my equilibrium, I replied, "I'll tell you what I *really* want, but I'm afraid you won't get it for me. I want a bottle of catsup!"

21

As the American stock market went dizzy in 1929, so did the price of Bunyore wives. Before the inflation, the standard price for a wife was five cows, four goats, and twenty-four shillings. But when U.S. Steel started to jump, so did Bunyore wives. For a while it was common to hear of a father asking as much as fourteen cows, four goats, and twenty-four shillings for his daughter; and settling for the unheard of price of ten cows, four goats, and twenty-four shillings.

Of course, Mother was partly responsible for this inflation, for the fathers argued, "If we pay money for our girls to attend the Bunyore Girls' School, why shouldn't we eat an extra cow or two?"

It was a good argument, but Dad didn't like it very well, for some of the fathers were using the church as a fulcrum to pry up the prices of their daughters. And this was a very easy thing to do. All the Christians longed for a church wedding. But if the father asked an unreasonable price for his daughter, it was frequently impossible to meet it—even on the installment plan. In the heathen system the groom was in a bargaining position, for he could elope with the girl, and thus ruin her value on the marriage market. But Christians, of course, refused to do this and the fathers—some of them professed Christians—saw their advantage and were ruthlessly taking it.

Mother dearly loved to help her girls prepare for their weddings. She helped them make their dresses and veils. The veils were made of netting and cut in such a way that they could be used for mosquito nets over the bed later on.

She also helped them bake a wedding cake, and I can remember her disgust when the bride's father, at a rather elaborate wedding, pinched out a handful of cake just before it was to be cut in front of the assembled guests. He had never eaten anything but *obusuma* and other native foods and didn't know any better.

"We've got to do something about this," said Dad just after the wedding plans of one of the mission girls had been ruined. "It isn't right that these fathers should be so unreasonable. The idea of a dowry isn't too bad. It helps guarantee the marriage, and it keeps the girls from marrying ne'er-do-wells. But too much is too much."

After months of prayer and thinking, the missionaries decided to suggest a price ceiling to the Church Council. In order to get this idea before the people, Dad called in some of the elders and discussed the problem with them. Some of these men had daughters in school and thus a bride-freeze would affect them directly. The problem was debated from every angle. They prayed over it. They discussed it with those

157

who were famous for being wise. Then they returned to the mission and announced that a maximum price should be set, and they suggested five cows, four goats, and twenty-four shillings.

Of course, in order to make this tentative agreement binding, it had to come before the Church Council. The day the measure was introduced, the assembly was packed, for the news had gotten around that the preachers were going to discuss how many cows a man could eat.

Dad explained the situation to the assembly, going over each point in great detail. Then he left the decision to them. The problem was discussed for three days without progress. "Let a man eat all the cows he can get," was the view taken by one man and shared by a host of others.

Another saw the matter in a different light. "No man should be allowed to eat more than three cows, four goats, and twenty-four shillings," he said, thumping his cane on the floor to emphasize his points. But he was not taken seriously, for he had just sold his daughter for ten cows.

The assembly was deadlocked. No one would budge, and all the missionaries were embarrassed. Mother wadded her handkerchief in her hands and prayed. The tension was getting tighter by the minute and trusted elders were making insinuating statements that would wrangle in the minds of others for years.

Then on the last day of the meeting, Musa (Moses), stood up.

"As you know," he said gravely, "I have a daughter in Mrs. Ludwig-i's Girls' School. She will finish this month, and her fees have cost me many shillings. Samwɾ'li, the son of Isaiah, is going to marry her. He has already brought me the dowry price of seven cows, four goats, and twenty-four shillings.

"But this problem that Bwana has been talking about has worried me many nights. We've got to do something about it. Some of you here can vote for a law to limit the number of cows a man can eat, and it won't hurt you because you have no daughters, or your daughters are already married. But this is not true with me. What I'm going to say will hurt my house,

158

for I have a son who will soon want to bring a wife, and he will need dowry cows.

"I think we should make a limit. And I think the limit should be five cows, four goats, and twenty-four shillings. And to prove that I really mean this, I will return two of Samwelli's cows. But as a reward for doing this, I want to be buried in a coffin and have a cement slab placed over my grave." There were tears in his eyes when he sat down, for he loved his herds. Five minutes later Musa's words were law. The vote was unanimous.

Dad pronounced the benediction. It was then that I knew that Musa's eyes were not the only ones that were swimming. The accusation that Christianity never got below a man's skin was not true!

Much encouraged by the action of the Church Council, Dad decided to go ahead with a cherished project he had had in mind for a long time. He remembered the words of the native who had said, "You white people have a yesterday, a today, and a tomorrow. We only have today and tomorrow, for all our parents are heathen." That statement bothered him when he first heard it, and it had continued to bother him. He knew how he had been helped by memories of the great events in American and church history. Frequently, in a trying situation, he had asked himself, What would Lincoln have done had he faced this problem? He began to pray that he would be able to find a tangible thing the Obunyores could point to as part of their yesterdays.

Their history, of course, was obscure. Then he thought of John Bila, the South African native who had given his all to Christ and then had died at Kima. He remembered the excellent words M. A. Baker had said about him. He knew that he would be a fine one to live in the memories of the people. He decided that he would find his grave and put a cement slab over it for people to visit and remember.

But who remembered where he was buried? Dad inquired, but the people shook their heads. They didn't know. He was determined, however, and soon he found some who had been at his funeral. The approximate place was staked out, a plain cement slab was poured and a suitable inscription made. Next, he poured slabs over the graves of the Kramer and Murray children beneath the wild olive tree at the corner of the mission.

After this he always felt a glow of satisfaction as he watched the natives pause and sometimes remove their hats before the graves. John Bila and the Kramer and Murray children were an indication that God had not completely forgotten them, even though Africa had been called the Dark Continent.

22

Christmas Day at Kima was a very special day, and the natives looked forward to it with childlike anticipation. None of them exchanged gifts or planned special meals. There was no deluge of Christmas cards, for such cards were unknown. The Obunyores considered it a great day because the early missionaries had taught them to celebrate it by bringing a special, sacrificial gift to Christ.

In preparation for the event, heavy offerings would be gathered by every pastor throughout the country. Many of the families would give an entire month's income and more. Then early on Christmas morning, sometimes long before sunrise if it were a distant village, the entire congregation, dressed in their best clothes, would assemble and start marching toward the mission. A skilled drummer—beating a drum strapped to the back of a young boy—would pound out the rhythms of the great songs of the church which they sang as they marched.

Listening from the veranda of the mission house, Mother would hear a group in the far distance singing "Standing on the Promises." "Well, there comes Danieli Aschiakhi and his congregation," she would predict, her face glowing. Then thinking of the spotless village with its wide streets and its stone church building seating more than six hundred, she would add, "What would we ever do without good old Danieli? He always stands behind the work, and some of our finest girls are from Es'salwa."

Then Dad would put a hand to his ear and quiet us with a loud shush. "Here comes another congregation," he would exclaim. "Listen! They're singing 'Onward Christian Soldiers.' I wonder who they are. Maybe it's Josephu Siminkha and his village. They sound like they're bringing a good offering."

The congregations would gather under the trees by the side of the foundations of the unfinished church building. Then the pastor of each village would bring the sack of money his people had collected, and place it on the wobbly table that stood before the missionaries.

On this particular Christmas we took our seats while the crowd seated itself on the grass. As Mother ran her eyes over the throng that numbered between ten and twenty thousand, she recognized a lot of the people. Many of them had been to the hospital or one of the schools, and as she looked at them, they smiled back. The line in front of the offering table glistened solidly with dazzling white *Americani* shirts and dresses. It was like the curved manual of a cathedral organ with all the black keys removed.

Then suddenly, just as the people were quieting, a little old man, naked except for his goatskin, walked boldly in front of the crowd and wedged himself between two enormously fat women right in front of Mother. Many in the crowd watched with angry eyes, but he didn't see them, for his face was toward Mother. "*Mirembe,* Mama!" he waved excitedly, smiling like a yawning hippopotamus.

It was then Mother recognized him. She nudged Miss Baker and whispered. "There's that little old man whose son forced him to come to the hospital after he'd gotten into a fight over his gardens. At first he didn't think he could become a Christian because he didn't have any clothes. But look at him now!"

Mother returned the wave. Encouraged, he got up, adjusted his goatskin so that it covered the front of his body, strode up to Mother and shook her hand, holding it in both of his. Then he said, "I want to thank you for telling me about Jesu Christo and for saving my life." As he returned to his place in the

161

crowd, he shifted the goatskin so that it covered the opposite side of his body.

The man's face shone with the power of the gospel, and glistened like highly polished leather. His presence must have inspired Dad, for he preached the best sermon on Ruth and Naomi—his usual subject at Christmas—that I had ever heard him preach.

Nevertheless, my mind wandered and I thought of another occasion when we had another unusually dressed visitor in a similar crowd at Ingotse. The visitor that day had on nothing but a huge pair of green goggles. Somehow or other Dad didn't see him until he got into the middle of the sermon. But after he had spotted him, it worked on his nerves. His preaching bogged down. He tried to look in another direction but he could not. He drank a glass of water. It didn't help. Finally, in utter desperation, he whispered to me, "Go tell that man to take off those goggles."

"But they're all he has on," I protested.

"Never mind," he replied. "You tell him to take them off!"

After the big crowd had been dismissed, I noticed a large group of natives standing in front of the unfinished church building. They were all looking straight up toward the sun, which, since it was noon, was hanging directly overhead. "What are you staring at?" I asked.

"There's a star shining by the sun," exclaimed a friend, grabbing me by the shoulder and excitedly pointed upward. "And, see, it's right over the big church!"

I followed his finger and he was right. There was a star just a few degrees from the sun. It seemed incredible, especially on a clear, brilliant day. But there it was. No one could deny it.

"This means that God wants us to finish the church building," announced a pastor who had been outspoken in opposition to allocating funds for its completion.

"I think he's right," put in another, quickly.

Soon this was the main topic of conversation. The enthusiasm grew, and by evening everyone seemed agreed the building should be completed. Calebu, the treasurer of the Christmas funds, expressed the consensus of opinion when he said, "It will be hard, but I think we can do it."

The missionary Christmas celebration started in our house at sunset that night. A small cedar tree had been cut and stood in the corner of our living room, and the Coleman lantern, now reserved for special days because it burned expensive gasoline, had been pumped up and glowed and hissed on the table in the center of the room.

All of the missionaries were present: the Murrays from Ingotse; Miss Baker; Rosalyn and Francis Paul from Kitale where they had purchased a farm; Mother, Dad, and myself. After a generous supper at which we feasted on a barbecued pig, raised and prepared by Mrs. Murray, we had our devotions and gathered around the tree.

Mother had discovered a few Christmas decorations, and so with a paper bell here, a lighted candle there, and some cedar branches on the bookcase and piano, the room had a real Christmas atmosphere. There was no Santa Claus, but Francis Paul more than made up for this. He cut holes in a square box, slipped it over his head as a mask, and with a generous portion of his ample Czech nose sticking out, clowned back and forth while he distributed the gifts.

The first gift was a glass car loaded with candy. This was for the Murrays who had been hoping for a better used car to enable them to visit more often in the villages. Mother received a fountain pen to take the place of the one she had worn out pleading money for the Bunyore Girls' School and hospital. Francis got a long pair of winter underwear conspicuously draped on the tree. This was an appropriate item, for nights around Kitale were cool. Everyone laughed as he draped them about him to see if they were the right size. Then he handed a card to Mother on which there was attached a long string.

A note on the card instructed her that she should follow this mysterious cord. She followed it to the door. Then, as she turned the knob, Mrs. Murray said, "You'd better get a light. There might be a leopard around. We saw some eyes when we drove over."

Mr. Murray produced a six-cell flashlight and all of us streamed outside to find the strange package that was apparently too large to be brought inside. Mother had been threatening to buy a donkey to ride around the mission and to Maseno, much to the horror of everyone, and I had a sinking feeling that this was the special gift. But I was mistaken.

The string led across the veranda, around the bougainvillae vine, and across some rose bushes to the base of a frangipani tree. And there, shining in the starlight, was a bathtub! It wasn't an enameled bathtub, but it was a bathtub! When Mother saw it, she cried, "Well, praise the Lord!" It had been presented by Rosalyn and Francis, and we all glowed with pride. The anticipation of taking a real hot bath in a permanent tub was warmly exhilarating to everyone.

Back in the living room, I waited, hoping for a present I could use. The small pile of packages kept diminishing, but none that was picked up had my name on it. I began to think that I was utterly forsaken like the hyena that was at that moment howling in the Bunyore Hills. But just as a lump started to form in my throat, I was handed a long package with my name written conspicuously on the brown wrapper.

As I removed the paper, I began to feel the shape of a bottle and my hopes soared. The Coleman lantern was now getting dim, and so Dad pumped it up with a series of enthusiastic thrusts. Then, just as the mantles were glowing at their maximum best, I got the last wrapper off. At that moment I had a surge of pure joy, for in my hand was a bottle of world-famous Heinz tomato catsup. That—along with a hammer and a gyroscope—was my Christmas. I was supremely happy.

But that night, just as I was drifting off to sleep, I was awakened by seeing Mother in the room. Dressed in her usual warm flannel nightgown, she stood at the end of the bed with a candle in her hand. I thought she had brought me some quinine, for Francis Paul had remarked during the evening that I was unusually white. But her empty hand showed that I was mistaken.

"Charles," she began, her eyes suddenly flooding and her voice breaking, "I-I'm sorry you didn't have a better Christmas." There was a long interval of silence as she struggled for control. Then she went on, "You're my only son, and I want you to know that both Dad and I love you with all our hearts. But we do have to keep the Girls' School and the hospital going. Maybe—maybe we can give you a better Christmas next year."

This emotional scene rather puzzled me. As far as I was concerned, I had had an excellent Christmas. A bottle of catsup? Well, a person didn't get a bottle of catsup every day. Especially Heinz catsup! As I went to sleep to the rhythm of the funeral drums, I felt a little guilty about the things I had said in regard to Mother neglecting me.

23

Mother rejoiced that the Christmas offering was over five thousand shillings, but when she learned the entire surplus would be used to help complete the church building instead of being given to her for the Bunyore Girls' School, she was keenly disappointed. "They could have given us at least five hundred shillings," she complained.

"But didn't you pray that the church building be completed before the rains wash the walls away?" asked Dad gently.

"Yes, I guess I did," she replied ruefully, her eyes on a distant village in the reserve where she knew there were girls who could not come to the school because there was no room.

"Well, God has answered one of your prayers and you should not be disappointed."

It was, however, a month of disappointments and disasters. A polite letter from the Government indicated they had no more funds for the school; the personal allowance check from the United States was cut by 30 percent; and the girls who cooked for us ran away because the men had told them they could never get married if they worked for white people.

Mother got the girls to come back by telling them the heart-rending story of her life and pointing out that she couldn't help the Africans if they didn't help her. She was so sincere and dramatic, they tearfully asked forgiveness and returned to work. But the money shortage continued.

The hospital ran out of bandages, and so Mother appropriated the sheets from our beds and any other white material that was available. Most of the personal allowance money was spent on *Americani* for bandages and for the always necessary quinine. She even made some of her own medicines, using honey, red peppers, the sap from blue gum trees, the fat from sheep tails, and a number of other things. I was always afraid that some of her concoctions would turn out to be poisonous or perhaps even explode. But my fears were for nothing. The medicine may only have been effective psychologically, but at least it did no harm. Moreover, her real dependence was upon the Lord, and hundreds of people were miraculously healed. In one year more than thirty thousand patients were treated.

Then some of the brightest students in the Boys' School decided they would go to another mission to finish their education. The other mission had large Government grants and excellent teachers. Mother had counted on these boys. She had hoped they would become teachers, evangelists, and pastors in our schools and churches. They were desperately needed, and she had spent countless hours in tutoring them so they could pass the Government examinations. Each time one of them announced his decision to leave, she would plead with him, sometimes in tears. But it did no good. Nevertheless, she held them up to the throne of grace and pled for each one by name.

A few, a very few returned. Sometimes it seemed to Mother that her prayers were just not getting through, that she was forsaken. At such times I would be instructed to play the record. She would listen to it several times and then retire to her room. There she would open the Bible to her favorite promises and pray until she was filled again with courage.

On top of these frustrations, she developed an illness that constantly drained her strength. This illness was in addition to her constant attacks of malaria. There were many times in her twenty-four hour days when she kept going merely through the strength of an outside energy. Each time we went to Kisumu,

Mother hoped for mail containing money for the work, or at least the promise of money. But each time she was disappointed.

The weevils, however, suffered no frustrations. They bored into the corn, devoured it from the inside, and multiplied. And their three trips to the football field each month seemed only to encourage them. Dad begged Mother to sell. I begged her to sell. Other missionaries begged her to sell. Native business-men begged her to sell. But she remained as firm as Gibraltar.

"I know that taxes are going to be collected soon," she said once after she had been unusually urged. "I know the workmen need to be paid, and some of them are beginning to think I deceived them. But I'm not going to sell until the price goes up, way up."

"But, Twyla," reasoned Dad, "everyone else has sold his corn. It's better to get something than nothing, and that's exactly what you're going to get."

"I've made up my mind," replied Mother, "and I won't change it. When the Lord tells me to sell the corn I'll sell it, and not until then!" She underlined her words by pursing her lips in the straightest line I'd ever seen.

Desperate to help, Dad built a steep tin chute with a heavy screen at the bottom. A fire was kindled under the screen and a couple of men were employed to shovel the corn down the chute where it hit the screen and shook a certain percentage of the weevils into the fire. This method helped, but again it was only temporary. One could still go by the laundry and hear them working.

But even more annoying than the near loss of the corn was the problem of constantly turning girls away from the school because there was no room. Mother had the dormitory beds placed together as closely as possible, had two girls assigned to each bed, and made use of every corner. In time the building began to resemble an overcrowded slaver. But the limits had been reached. There was not room for another girl.

Mother considered each girl a potential evangelist for Christ, and the loss of training irreparable. Her frustrations touched all of us, for she was constantly speaking about the role women would play in the New Africa. We heard about the Girls' School during all the daylight hours, and at night we were kept awake by her prayers or the scratch of her pen as she wrote letters to America pleading for help.

24

Mother eagerly scooped up the mail at the Kisumu post office, laid it on the worn lorry seat, and began to sort it. Several ships must have come in, for the stack was unusually thick.

Having suffered a severe siege of malaria and a horrible time of weakness from the other illness, she hoped she would find a letter that would send her spirits soaring. Dad had been predicting that someone would send them seven thousand dollars. Perhaps this was the day! She quickly pushed aside a letter from Fern and a crudely addressed envelope she knew to be from her mother. The good news, she felt, would be in the long brown envelope from the Board.

For a long time she had been praying, trusting in "the Promises," and exercising faith for money to operate the mission and start new projects. The Lord had sold their farm without advertising at a generous profit; he had healed her when the doctors said she would die; and he had opened the way for them to come to Kenya. An almost electric confidence assured her that stimulating news was in the mail before her on the seat.

The letter from the Missionary Board had been folded inside the Bushnell paper, and thus she did not find it until all the mail had been sorted. She opened it with great assurance and began to read. Then her spirits sagged. The burden of the three-page mimeographed letter was an explanation of why in those depression times they were receiving only half their salary that month.

Mother thrust the epistle from herself as if it were a snake. She, too, had read of the eleven million Americans out of work, of the long bread lines, of farm foreclosures, of ruined fortunes. But she thought of the mission's need of bandages and quinine.

Mohammed brought her thoughts back from the girls in the Bunyore villages to Kisumu by placing a bottle of rose on the table at her elbow. She had a large unpaid bill for *Americani* at this store, and she hated to increase it without making at least a token payment. But the hospital had to have bandages and so she ordered another bolt, promising to pay as soon as possible. Somehow or other the money would come.

With her bulging pocketbook in hand, its strap held together with a safety pin, she went from place to place ordering supplies. Sometimes the Indian storekeepers had reluctant faces because the account was overdue, but each time they gave her what she wanted and she signed the bill. Delinquent accounts were a great trial to Dad, but his grumbling was kept to a minimum because he knew the hospital and Girls' School had to go on. Moreover, he believed the money would be supplied. But when?

The lorry cab on the way back to Kima was like a chamber of gloom. Neither Mother nor Dad had had a vacation for several years; both of them were taking quinine every day, and each one had been near to blackwater fever. The pessimistic letter from the Board seemed to trigger all their suppressed fears, anxieties, and frustrations. As they were climbing the escarpment they passed a man dressed in a long-tail coat and stovepipe hat, but without any trousers. The unusual sight failed to bring even a smile to either one.

Mother was especially discouraged because her prayers seemed not to be getting through. She searched her mind for some disobedience or lack of consecration. "I know the Board is trying to do the best it can," she said as they drew near Maseno. "And I know the churches are not all backslidden or cold. It's just that they don't know. I wish I could be ten people all at once. If I could, I'd go up and down the land and by the time I'd get through, the churches would either be giving to missions or I would know the reason why!"

On the other side of Maseno, they came to a man carrying

an enormous pile of wood on his head. "John," said Mother, "let's stop and pick him up."

Dad stopped and the man placed his wood on the lorry and then climbed in. But after he had seated himself, he replaced the wood on his head again and kept it in that position until he got to his village. Mother watched him with amusement. Then her brown eye and blue eye lit up with the fiercest light they had had for days.

"You know, I think that God sent him to teach us a lesson," she said, her voice wrapped in an almost ecstatic joy. "We've been groaning under all these mission problems for nothing. David said, 'Cast thy burden on the Lord, and he shall sustain thee.' From this time on that's what I'm going to do." Dad, also, must have felt a great relief from this lesson, for he forgot to change gears and continued on into the mission in second even though gasoline was still seventy-five cents a gallon.

Samwelli and I were enjoying a meal of flying ants when I noticed several red clouds approaching from the north. "What's that?" I asked pointing to the spiraling masses.

Samwelli's eyes followed my finger. Then his eyes fell as if he had just heard of the death of a loved one. "The locusts are coming!" he muttered with clenched hands. "They will ruin our gardens. The land will be as bare as a woman's head. What will we ever do? There will be a famine!"

The locusts came and there was nothing that could be done. There were millions of them—no, tens and hundreds of millions. When they crossed the sky at noon the country was shrouded in darkness. They settled in the trees, and eight-inch branches were snapped like matchsticks. A garden would be green one day and as bare as a boulder the next. Trains were stalled, the wheels slipping on the crushed locusts. Our car made tracks wherever it went, red tracks of dead locusts.

The natives went after them with clubs, but it was like trying to chop down a baobab tree with a broken straw. Before you had killed a dozen, a hundred more came to take their places. The Government recruited armies of men to destroy them, but they didn't know where to begin.

Samwelli, like everyone else, went out with a bag and gathered them by the thousands. "If the locusts eat our gardens, we will eat the locusts," he said grimly. I went with him. A bushel basket could be filled to the brim in less than five minutes. All we had to do was to hold the basket under a limb and shake the limb. During the day one could hear them eating, and their millions of jaws working together sounded like a heavy wind blowing through telegraph wires. We gathered them until we ached. Then we lugged them over to Samwelli's house and crammed them into a bag which we immersed in boiling water. Then we pulled off the wings and legs and placed the finger-length bodies in a basket.

The next day we spread the dead locusts over the top of a large boulder so the sun could shine on them and dry them out. After a week of drying, they were stored away until needed. The natives prepared them to eat by either roasting or frying and serving with salt. They tasted like crisp bacon, and I enjoyed them even more than raw ants. But when I brought a heaping plate to Mother, she refused to taste even one. "I don't think you're much of a missionary if you won't even eat a locust," I taunted.

Finally her resistance broke down and she picked up the smallest one on the plate. But instead of popping it into her mouth and eating it without question, she pulled the head off. Unfortunately the inside mechanisms stuck to the head, and the sight wasn't pretty. I begged her to eat just the head, but she wouldn't. I told her they were delicious, that locusts only ate vegetables, that John the Baptist ate locusts, that she didn't know what she was missing. But it was a waste of time.

The vast swarms of locusts stayed. Neither whistles nor clubs nor poison could get rid of them. The Obunyores became desperate about their crops, and the price of corn began to climb. The Government stepped in and bought up all the available corn in order to feed the hungry people.

Mother sold her corn for twelve shillings a bag and thus cleared nine hundred dollars profit. "See what the Lord has done!" she exclaimed. "Now we'll pay off our debts and build a new building that will take care of another twenty girls!"

"Do you mean the Lord sent the locusts in order to raise the price of corn so that you could make a few dollars?" I asked.

"No, I don't think the Lord sent the locusts to raise the price of corn," she replied thoughtfully. "But I do think the Lord knew the price would go up, and he helped us to get the corn so that we would be ready when it did go up."

25

Shortly after the corn was sold, the British Government put Mother on salary with the understanding the money would be used for the Bunyore Girls' School. This sent her enthusiasm and confidence to new heights. The Lord had confirmed his Word, and she began to view new and distant peaks.

"Isn't it wonderful how God keeps his promises!" she exulted as she poured Dad a cup of tea on the day she received the good news.

"Yes, it's marvelous," he agreed, nervously watching the teapot. "But it's also wonderful the way he obeys his own laws. The law of gravity, for instance. Twyla, if you tip that pot any higher, you'll break another lid!"

Mother's mind, however, was higher than Kilimanjaro, and she didn't seem to hear him. The pot handle went up and up. The lid came out and balanced precariously on the edge. Then it plopped back in place and Dad sighed with relief. Ndosio filled the pot again as Mother dreamed on. But this time Dad took charge. They couldn't afford new teapots every week even though the corn had sold at a profit and the Government was sending a grant.

Mother finished her tea, and Dad lifted the pot to refill her cup. But at that precise moment, she said, "John, let's write to the Building and Loan in Omaha, get our savings, and put them in the work." This thought was such a shock to him, the pot fell from his hand, struck the cement, and shattered into a hundred pieces.

172

"And what will we live on when we're old?" he asked, surveying the wreckage.

"God will take care of us. He has the cattle on a thousand hills!"

In time the money was withdrawn and every cent was put in the work. The Girls' School grew and the routine of the mission continued. Each year new congregations were established, and each year Dad baptized five or six hundred new converts. The locusts departed, new buildings were built, and Mother began to make use of every available inch of mission land to raise vegetables and corn to help feed the girls and keep the operating costs down.

Luka watched the girls' sweet potatoes grow with great interest and each day secretly licked his lips. In time he could resist the temptation no longer and began to dig a few for his supper. He had just placed two rather large ones in a basket when Dad came along.

"Why, Luka, I'm surprised that you would steal sweet potatoes," he said, teasing him.

"Bwana Ludwig-i, I'm not stealing. It's daylight. Thieves only steal after the sun has gone to bed."

"Is that so?"

"Yes, that is the way it is, Bwana," confirmed the old man, nodding his head like a thoughtful elephant.

"Well, you have taught me a new word," said Dad, going over to Luka's house and picking up his pet rooster. "I think I'll take him home and have Ndosio cook him for supper."

Luka ran after him as he started toward the house. "You're stealing my rooster!" he shouted, a mixture of terror and sorrow in his creaky voice.

"No, I'm not stealing," replied Dad, after he had locked the squawky bundle of red feathers in the coop. "It's all right to take anything you want to take regardless of who it belongs to, provided you take it while the sun's out of bed."

"Oh, please, Bwana, give it back," begged Luka mournfully. "You've taught me a lesson, and I won't dig any more of the

173

mission's sweet potatoes." The rooster was returned and Luka kept his word.

In 1938, after eleven years of almost uninterrupted work, Mother and Dad returned to the United States on furlough. A throng of natives crowded into the mission to see them off. Among these was the little old man who had been wounded in the garden fight. Taking Mother's hand in both of his, he said, "Good-bye, Mama. It may be that when you return I will no longer be here. But if that is so, I'll see you up there." He pointed to the sky. As he turned from her, he covered his bareness by shifting his goatskin. His eyes swam with tears.

The furlough was supposed to be a time of rest. Instead, it was a period of tremendous activity. Every minute was scheduled in advance. Major surgery for Mother had priority. There was not a moment to lose, for her problem was gradually ruining her health. A number of people who knew of her healing and of her success in praying for the healing of others, were greatly alarmed that she would submit to surgery. Her position in this matter was explained in a letter she sent to America a number of years later:

"Many who profess to believe the truthful promises of God and who think they are standing for them, are not standing for them at all. Refusing doctors, medicine, and medical skill is not *divine* healing. Some people let their loved ones suffer, thinking they are trusting in God. . . . Divine healing is God . . . coming into a room, whatever that place may be, and actually laying his powerful divine hand upon whatever circumstance that is foreign to his will, and rebuking it and changing the circumstances."

Mother felt that her progress with the Bunyore Girls' School was hindered because she did not have a college degree. She presented her credits to Dean Russell Olt at Anderson College and discovered that if she worked hard she could complete her bachelor's degree in one year. Mother attacked this work with a new vitality. She and I took some classes together, but her grades were always higher than mine. In due course she was

174

graduated. But I think she felt a little guilty in spending this time in school, and so she filled up her extra moments with speaking engagements and in writing *Polished Pillars,* a booklet about the Girls' School. This publication became a favorite, and she used the earnings from the six editions to build new buildings for the girls.

One of the speaking engagements led her to Portsmouth, Ohio. There a little lad by the name of David Livingston listened attentively. Mother was intrigued by his name and interest. With a peculiar inspiration, she laid her hands on his head and prayed that God would make him into a medical missionary who would serve in Kenya. And later, whenever she thought of him, she sent a prayer to the throne of grace that this prayer might be fully answered.

She and Dad traveled for a while in different directions in order that they might tell more people about the needs of Africa. She inspired relatives and friends and congregations to take on building projects, and everywhere she went she urged young people to consider the mission field. But she warned them that they should not go unless they received a divine call.

Still one thing needed to be done. There were fine clays around Kima that could be used for a flourishing pottery business—a business that would help the native economy. But the traditional way of making pots there was too crude and slow to be really effective. There was only one solution, and that was to learn the proper methods herself and then pass them on.

Investigation showed that an excellent course on this subject was taught at Tuskegee Normal and Industrial Institute in Tuskegee, Alabama. When Mother announced her intentions to attend this school, her friends shook their heads. "But that's a school for Negroes!" they exclaimed, amazed that she would even consider attending such a place.

But the fact that it was a Negro school interested Mother all the more. There she would learn new methods of dealing with colored people, and gain new insights into their psychology. Moreover, she would meet illustrious Negroes whom she could hold up as models to the Bunyore. No longer would she have to search her brain to suggest a name for the new baby born at one o'clock in the morning.

As she settled in the train that would take her to Alabama, she felt a warm glow of satisfaction. Things were working out in a marvelous way. New buildings had been promised. Bright-eyed young people had felt the call to be missionaries and were preparing themselves, and she had a strange assurance that young David Livingston would actually become a Kenya doctor. Later in the day, she spent some time praying for the girls in the school and then drifted off to sleep.

Her sleep was rudely interrupted by the gruff voice of the conductor who called out sharply, "Ticket please!"

Mother, much to the amusement of the people across the aisle, could not find the elusive piece of parchment. She felt the conductor's eyes glowering at her and was certain he felt she was trying to put one over on him. In desperation, she decided to empty her pocketbook on the seat. This monstrosity had grown until it was at least a foot thick. When she opened it, it was like opening one of Ali Baba's battered treasure chests. The conductor stood goggle-eyed as she emptied it. First there was a razor and a box of face powder; then a pair of scissors and adhesive tape; next an address book, a dictionary, a New Testament, and a book on pottery; several spools of thread, a heavy comb, and an envelope full of stamps. The contents were almost endless.

But finally, as always, she produced the ticket. It had been mixed up with the stamps. The conductor studied it for a full minute in complete silence. Then he said, "Are *you* going to Tuskegee?"

"That's right. I'm going to take a special course from Dr. Hathaway."

"Tuskegee is a school for Negroes, isn't it?" he continued, staring at her brown curly hair and brown eye.

"Yes, of course. It was founded by Booker T. Washington."

"Then Ah'm afraid M'am, Ah'm going to have to ask you to move to another carriage. This one is reserved for whites!" His voice was coldly polite.

Mother had never been mistaken for a Negro before, but she was delighted and moved in with the colored people at once. This was a good story to tell, and she enjoyed every part of it. Down at the Institute she became a close friend of George Washington Carver. The two of them used to meet together and pray for a New Africa. When it came time for her to leave, Dr. Carver arranged her transportation to the station. The memory of his great spirit was one of the treasures she took back to Kenya.

In September of 1940 Mother and Dad completed their arrangements to sail for Africa. Because of the war, the only ship available was a freighter jammed with war materials—mostly ammunition and army trucks. They were the only passengers. But Mother rejoiced that a way—any way—had been opened for their return, and she was particularly happy because of the many boxes of equipment they were taking back with them. This equipment included an item of special joy for her, a real, properly built delivery table. The old table of pine crates could now take a long deserved rest!

Because of the fear of submarines—one torpedo would be enough—and because the ship stopped at many ports, the trip lasted for three months. After boat drill the captain liked to remind Mother that a lone woman on board could be a bad omen, and that if they got into serious trouble he would be obliged to throw her overboard.

Dad occupied his time with a fishing line. But although he put all his efforts into it, he could not get a single nibble. Nevertheless, he remained at the prow of the ship refusing to give up. The crew marveled at his patience and suggested various kinds of bait.

On the day before they were scheduled to land at Mombasa, he handed the pole to Mother while he went into their cabin in search of a book. He had just disappeared through the door when Mother got a bite and reeled in a three-pounder. This made the Captain so mad he swore, and, wagging a finger in Mother's face, he stormed, "Something told me I should have thrown you overboard at Capetown!"

As Mother and Dad prepared to leave the ship, a native came on board with a large bouquet of pink carnations beautifully tied with ribbons like a bridal bouquet. Attached to the flowers was a letter from the Church Council, welcoming them back to Kenya. The Captain looked at it and turned aside. His seafaring eyes filled with tears. "I have been sailing the seas for many years," he said, "and I have carried many missionaries back and forth from their various fields. This is the first time I have ever seen such a thing." Mother was so overwhelmed she couldn't speak.

The Bunyore Girls' School had made some progress during the furlough period. But with Mother's new equipment, additional funds, and increased enthusiasm, the work shifted into high gear. Again sewing machines hummed during the small hours of the morning and visions became realities.

Getting the girls through the Government examinations so that they could be teachers was unusually hard. The girls had been taught for endless generations that they were inferior to the men, and it was hard to break this complex. Moreover, the boys would come close to their dormitories and taunt them. "You can't pass the examinations," they would sneer. "A woman's brains aren't much better than a goat's!" Sometimes they even sent letters. "Don't you dare pass. We don't want you to be as wise as we are. We won't marry you if you pass."

In the beginning there were many failures in the literary subjects even though most of them passed in domestic science. Frequently the girls knew enough answers to pass, but their brains would go dead because of the taunts of the boys and community. In 1944 only three girls passed in everything, but each girl was from a different tribe: Marigole, Bunyore, and Kipsigis.

Mother exulted in the girls that were graduated, but the girls themselves suffered humiliation from the boys who called them every imaginable vile name, including "white people" and "old maids." Nevertheless, this prejudice gradually broke down, and more and more of the girls passed the examinations and became qualified teachers, nurses, and domestic servants.

One of the great needs of the school was an adequate domestic science building. The Government grants had been increased each year, but there was not enough money to complete such a building. Mother knew there was one certain way to get it, and that was to have a series of sales. This time she decided to have a mammoth one right in the heart of Nairobi. The announcement of this plan sent girls' hearts fluttering. Nairobi! . . . Perhaps seeing the Governor! . . . The whole idea was so marvelous they could hardly stand even to think about it.

Naomi Allan, in Belfast Ireland, had grown burdened for the Bunyore Girls' School, and she began to send Mother linen mill-ends and scraps discarded by the textile mills. These were made into tablecloths, napkins, and other useful items. The girls worked on them for months. The thoughts of the new building and Nairobi kept their eyes open through the small hours of the mornings. Mother wrote:

"It was a big venture for us to hold a sale in Nairobi. Even I had been there only a few times before. The teachers and I . . . decided I should write to a well-known man we knew in Nairobi and ask him to arrange a place for us. Nevertheless, we labored on with little thought of the place, expecting any day to hear that a suitable one had been found.

"For a week we washed and ironed the linen we had sewed, and we packed it carefully in the trunks that were to go to Nairobi. The day before the lorry was to come to Kima for the trunks, we were doing the final things: toy dogs were being stuffed and sewed up, cushions were getting their backs on them, buttons were being sewed on the sweaters that had been knitted. . . . Then I was handed a telegram: HAVE SEARCHED EVERYWHERE FOR PLACE FOR SALE. IT CANNOT BE FOUND.

"It was nine o'clock in the evening. The stoves were hot. Everyone, happily expectant, looked into my face to hear the report of the telegram, but kept on ironing or whatever her work happened to be. I steadied myself for a moment. Then I read the telegram aloud. When I had finished, I turned the lantern low and said, 'Let us pray.' In Olinyore I laid the whole

179

situation before the Lord: the great need of the new building, the need for trained African women, the need for changed African homes. . . . Then I asked the Lord to guide us as to what to do.

"After saying, 'amen,' I turned up the light and got up from my knees, looked at the teachers who were present, and said, 'Well, girls, what does the Lord lead you to do?'

" 'Let us go by faith,' they replied in one voice.

" 'Amen, let us go,' I replied.

"We worked all night. At daylight we were ready for the lorry. Miss Baker sent me a lovely tray of tea. I shall never forget how good it was. . . . I was so tired that the minute I boarded the train I lay down on the seat and went to sleep. I did not stop for tea or food of any kind. But whenever I would awake, I would cry out for a place for a sale. About eight o'clock that evening a missionary from Tanganyika came with her child to spend the night in my compartment. I told her my burden, and we agreed together before the throne of grace that a place would be supplied in due time."

At Nairobi, Mother hired a *jinricksha* and as the native runner, monkey fur on his knees and ankles, pulled her down Government Road, the girls followed with huge bundles of sales items on their heads. It was an utterly fantastic sight. Some of the older people must have been reminded of Tippu Tib returning from the interior with a column of slaves.

But each time Mother stopped at a business house and begged for space to have her sale, she was politely refused. She went up and down the streets for a room or a few empty counters, but with no results. There just wasn't any room anywhere for the sale.

Finally, when she was so exhausted she could hardly move, she stopped in Jack Frost's ice-cream parlor for a minute of rest. "I went back in the corner and sat down behind a little table and began to pray with all my heart. I laid the whole matter before God and asked him to guide me to where I could have the sale." Then, after reading some promises, Mother introduced herself to a very beautiful little lady known as

Frankie. Frankie listened to her story and suggested that she see A. L. Block, the manager at Bullows and Roy.

Mr. Block, who was also the owner of the famed Norfolk Hotel, listened carefully as Mother related her needs. Then he said, "I'll discuss it with my committee. You come back at five and I'll give you their answer."

Mother returned to the ice-cream parlor and told Frankie the results of her visit. "This is all nonsense!" she exclaimed, rubbing her expressive hands together. "Mr. Block is his own director. You go and tell him you want the shop *now!*"

Mother went back with a new determined fire smoldering in her brown eye and blue eye, and this time Mr. Block agreed that she could use the store and pointed out a spacious room with plenty of tables. She then rushed an ad into the *East African Standard,* and the next day the sale was officially underway. The white people of Nairobi were enthusiastic and opened their pocketbooks. A typical comment was: "You don't mean to say that this work has all been done by native girls, do you? It looks more like European work."

The sale netted $1,100.00. The Government then added another $4,500.00 and Dad built the new domestic science building.

26

The next ten years were the happiest years in Mother's life. The Bunyore Girls' School had passed its major hurdles and the Government was responding with more and more support. The graduates were becoming the wives of leading ministers, teachers, evangelists, businessmen, and Government workers. The villages for miles around were hearing the gospel, learning better ways to live, and building better homes. Some of the girls were even operating their own businesses. Daudi's daughter, Ramona, had a bakery at Kakamega and was selling over a thousand loaves of bread a day. She baked them in a clay oven Mother had developed from the knowledge she gained at Tuskegee.

The funeral horns continued to blow, but with much less

frequency. David Livingston had enrolled in medical school and had been accepted for assignment in Kenya by the Missionary Board.

A new mission had been founded at Kisa, and the number of congregations had grown from forty-nine to an impressive one hundred and nine. Moreover, new and substantial Government grants were coming in for various mission projects each year.

Mother and Father returned to the United States for their second furlough. Both of them were convinced their work was just beginning. But the Board felt otherwise. Since Father was over sixty-five, they had reached the standard retirement age. This was a bitter blow to Mother. She thought of new advancements for the Bunyore Girls' School, of new villages to be reached for Christ.

For two years she wrestled with the thoughts of a pensioned retirement. "You have worked hard enough, you deserve a rest," suggested many of her friends. But she had a restlessness in her bones that could not be satisfied in America. The horrors of suffering African women were constantly before her. Finally she made up her mind. She would return to Africa and give her last ounce of strength for Christ even if she had to go out on her own. It was a hard and painful decision to make, but it was one she never regretted. She was determined to die in Africa.

Her new sphere of labor, Mother decided, would be in or around Nairobi. She and Dad parked their little twelve-foot trailer in the Public Park at Nairobi and began to pray for directions. While they waited on the Lord, they visited natives in the public hospitals and wrote to their American friends who were standing behind them financially. Then, as they were drinking tea at the Norfolk, their old friend, A. L. Block, came in and joined them at their table.

Mother told him of her dreams to start a new school for girls in that area. As always, the magic of her words and the glow of her brown eye and blue eye captivated him. He, too, could see the need of the school. After a little thought, he presented her with ten acres of land in the Ruarka Estates just nine miles from the city. She and Dad went out to claim it with the enthusiasm Abraham enjoyed when he stepped into the Promised Land.

The land was completely bare. There was no water or electricity. But this made no difference to Mother's imagination. To a friend she wrote: "God has opened up a place for us . . . which is very unique in its possibilities. For this we thank our friends who have continued to hold us up in prayer to the Father who has truly answered in a great way; to the northeast the Government has been building up a large military camp where several hundred African boys from various parts of Kenya are in training for military service. We want to give them interesting programs from time to time where we can show films of a religious nature, which may lend an influence on their lives. . . . They need his help more than I can possibly indicate in this brief letter. To the northwest are brick and tile factories, where many more Africans are employed. Some of these natives have their families with them. Many have come from their native reserves and have become skilled workmen. Little is being done to educate their children. . . .

"To the east, directly in front of us is a large sugar cane plantation with a sugar factory where more Africans are employed. And to the south and west are fourteen stone quarries where another five hundred men are employed."

In addition to all of this, Mother rejoiced that on a clear day the snows of both Mount Kenya and Mount Kilimanjaro could be seen. With this exotic setting she began to build buildings and plan for another girls' school. She believed she had at least another twenty years of life to give, and was determined that every second and even split-second count.

She wrote: "I am more convinced than ever before that the condition Kenya is in today can only be corrected as we work with God . . . through faith in the blood of the Lord Jesus Christ which was shed on Calvary as the only remission of sins. . . . Every condition laid out by Paul to Timothy concerning the conditions of the people in the last days is represented here. The form of religion has failed to bring about the changed lives required to bring forth a change necessary to transform lives whose background is one of sin: lies, adultery, deception, cunningness, and hypocrisy. . . .

Building after building was won through prayer. Dad had a well put down and excellent water was found at five hundred feet. He purchased a tractor and began to raise his own vegetables. Mother planted flowers, and the new mission became a rainbow of color. In order to get students for the new school, which she had named Domestic Science School for African Girls, she ran ads in the *East African Standard*. With an excellent reputation throughout Kenya as a leading educator of women, she had no difficulty in getting girls for the school. They came from many tribes: Obunyore, Kikuyu, Kipsigis, Swahili, and the Wakamba. A hymnal of some of the great hymns of the church was produced with the words printed in these various languages. It was heartwarming to see the girls and their families and friends from these formerly warring tribes sitting side by side in the little aluminum church building and singing together: "The Church Has One Foundation."

When money was slow in coming in, Mother arranged for sales. The Nairobi businessmen cooperated, and she was given the use of some of the finest buildings in the city. Also, many of the white women, who worked as secretaries or clerks in the downtown stores, gave up their lunch hours in order to help price the various items and get the displays ready.

Once again Mother was in the whirl of night and day work. She was supremely happy. Then the headlines in the papers bled with the sinister words: Mau Mau. The first victim of this secret organization, determined to drive the white man from Kenya, was a woman. She was brutally hacked to death one half mile from the mission. Then two European boys were murdered two miles went of the mission. Next one hundred Kikuyu: men, women, and children, were chopped to bits at Lari.

The great mystery was that the normally kind Kikuyu could do such things. "A Kikuyu leading an apparently normal life would, in one moment, become a being that was barely human. A most notable manifestation of this was the murder of the

184

Ruck family at the end of 1953. Mr. Ruck's groom, who led a gang of terrorists, enticed Mr. Ruck from his house at night on a spurious statement that a gangster had been arrested. He was battered to death in front of his wife who had come out to assist him, and she was then murdered. On the instructions of the groom, their small son, aged six, hiding in terror in the house, was then slashed to death—a typical Mau Mau murder. The groom who led the attack, had only a few days previously carried the boy tenderly home some miles from the house after a riding accident."[1]

The reason these men did these things was, of course, because of the Mau Mau oath. This oath was designed to violate every human and Christian decency.

The basic promises of the oath were as follows:

If I am sent to bring the head of an enemy or a European, and I fail to do so, may this oath kill me.
If I fail to steal anything from a European, may this oath kill me.
If I know of an enemy of our organization, and I fail to report it, may this oath kill me.
If I am ever sent by my leader to do something big for the House of Kikuyu, and I refuse, may this oath kill me.
If I worship any leader but Jomo Kenyatta, may this oath kill me.[2]

This oath, taken under the most dramatic and revolting conditions, had a stranglehold on its victims. In order to increase this hold, new depths of savage variations to the oathing ceremony were constantly developed. Some of the ceremonies that evolved were so terrible they are completely unprintable.

Many a trusted Kikuyu turned out to be an oath-giver, and many a white person—even those who had been unusually kind to the natives—were slaughtered by the Mau Mau. Death lurked behind every tree, both for the whites and the loyal natives—especially Christians.

Mother's friends advised her to lock the mission and move to Nairobi for better protection. But such a move, as far as she was concerned, was beyond consideration. Almost every white

[1]Official Government Reports, "The Origin and Growth of Mau Mau," p. 9.
[2]*Ibid.*, p. 166.

person in the country carried a gun. When the women at one of her sales opened their purses to get their money, they often had to fumble beyond a loaded revolver. But neither Mother nor Dad would keep a gun in the house.

"The Mau Mau will get you one of these nights," warned some of the terror-stricken whites. "You ought to at least have a gun handy. . . ."

But Mother was steadfast in her refusal, and Dad said, "If the Mau Mau want to kill me, I'll be waiting. Heaven is only one step away." Guns, Mother decided, could jam or miss. The Word of God never jammed and never missed. She kept a Bible by her bedside and trusted in the Lord. In childlike faith, both she and Dad snored until the windows rattled.

Frantic letters from me never disturbed them. They believed they were in God's will and, "If God be for us, who can be against us" (Rom. 8:31)? Many people fled the country, including some missionaries. But Mother said, "God has called us to a work, and through his grace and wisdom and wealth we're going to finish it!" She always completed this statement with her lips in as firm a line as any Mau Mau *panga*.

Just before the opening of school one morning, a Kikuyu drove an old truck into the mission and called for Mother. He presented her with a half a bag of corn and a half a bag of potatoes. "This," he said gravely, "is to show that we know that you are our friend. It is a sign that we will never harm you."

Later, as she was riding to Nairobi on a bus, a young British soldier, wearing his green battle dress and sitting across the aisle, said, "I know you, Mrs. Ludwig, and I know all about your work."

"But I don't know you," she replied, summoning all her strength to close her pocketbook which was now considerably more than a foot thick.

"Every night you take a lantern at dusk," he replied with a boyish smile, "and go out and check all the locks on the buildings. Then you return to the mission house."

"How do you know all this?" asked Mother, fixing him with her brown eye and blue eye.

"Oh, that's easy. The Government is concerned about you. They have posted me by one of the trees near the mission. I often sit there and guard you with a machine gun!"

Mother was glad to have made his acquaintance. But she took his work as a matter of course. God had promised to look after her. Experience had shown that he always kept his word!

27

In 1958 I flew to Kenya to participate in my parents' fiftieth wedding anniversary on November 5. As I landed at the airport, I visualized a week of intense visiting with both of them. There were so many things to talk about, but as I walked eagerly toward them, I little knew how mistaken I was.

Mother had my schedule all worked out. Every second had been budgeted for some useful occupation. Most of my time was to be spent with Dad, for she felt he wouldn't be with us very long. She, herself, was tied up in the city getting ready for another sale. The anniversary "wedding," she informed me, would be in the salesroom.

"But, Mother, you can't have a golden wedding celebration in a salesroom!" I objected, my mouth sagging in horror.

"Oh, yes, we can," she replied, reaching for a nail file in her seemingly expectant pocketbook. "A lot of our friends will come to the wedding. And there is no reason why they shouldn't buy some of the fancywork and help our school!"

The week before an eager young man, who wanted to be a missionary, had landed at Nairobi. On inquiry, he was told that if he *really* wanted to become a missionary, he should call on the Ludwigs. Without the slightest knowledge of what he was really getting into, the unfortunate man presented himself to Mother, saying, "I'm here to help you. I'll do anything you ask me to do. I want to learn to be a missionary."

When I heard what he had done, I laughed until I shook. My life with Mother had taught me to disappear whenever a sale or special project was underway. Getting into her clutches when work was to be done, was like sticking one's head in a lion trap. But he wanted good training, and Mother decided she would be a good teacher.

He had come just in time to get the salesroom ready for the big day. After he had worked with Mother nearly all night for two nights in a row, he was groggy from want of sleep. But Mother kept him going in the same way she kept herself going, by telling him the great needs of the school, and by filling him with enormous quantities of scalding *Simba Chai*. She stoked him with tea in the same way Dad had stoked the thrashing machine on his Illinois farm.

Lunching with me in a stolen moment, he said, "I have been in the Army and Air Force, and never have I seen a personality as strong as your mother's. Talk about shin-kicking sergeants. They don't know where to begin! She sent me to get some potatoes. I went to a dozen stores and couldn't find any. When I told her this, she said, 'Don't give up until you go to *every* store in Nairobi.'

"I went to nearly every store in Nairobi, but I still couldn't find any. When I told her that, she said, 'You go get them *anyway*.' 'But, Mrs. Ludwig,' I replied, 'there just aren't any. Do you want me to grow some?'

" 'I don't care how you get them,' she answered, banging her fist on the table, 'but you must get them. And you must get them right away.' " He got them!

At the anniversary wedding, the salesroom was comfortably filled with friends. Rosalyn sang "O Promise Me." Then I faced Mother and Dad, the slender black wedding book in my hands. Remembering all the extra questions Mother used to ask at native ceremonies, I was carefully prepared.

"Do you promise to obey?" I asked sternly, facing Mother.

"I do," she replied, nodding her head vigorously.

"But do you promise to obey in everything?"

"Yes, everything."

"Are you sure?" I continued, pressing home the best advantage I had ever had in my life.

"I'm sure."

188

I then pronounced them "man and wife" and insisted they kiss each other. Then we children put our money together and rented them a room in the Norfolk. Mother agreed they would use the room, *provided* she had the privilege of working late on the sale.

The progress of the Ruarka Mission was an amazing revelation to me. Twenty-two buildings had already been constructed. There was a fine stone mission house, the garden was full of vegetables, the dormitory was full of girls, and plans for further progress were everywhere. That two people beyond retirement age and facing all kinds of handicaps, illness, and the lack of funds could accomplish so much was an indication of the power of God and singleness of purpose.

Always when Mother told of her call to Africa, her voice choked and her eyes overflowed. "The Lord gave me a vision of heaven," she would declare, "and it was real, very real . . . I saw the glory of it, and it is worth everything. Everything!" This was a subject on which none of the rest of us ever commented. It seemed too incredible. Likewise, George Frideric Handel's servant was a little dubious when his bankrupt master got up from his desk after having written the "Hallelujah Chorus" and with tears in his eyes declared, "I did think I did see all heaven before me, and the great God himself." But when people listened to the *Messiah*, they knew it was true. In the same way, when I thought of Mother's achievements in Africa, I *knew* that her vision was true.

Our last moments together were at the airport as the big BOAC airliner taxied down the runway. Suddenly she remembered something. She hurried upstairs to the tourist shop. Five minutes later she returned with a crocodile belt for my son, Charles, and a zebra belt for my daughter, Brenda. "Tell them" she said, "that these are from their old Granny and Grandpa."

Mother soon came to the last great enthusiasm of her life. One of her girls worked in the home of an American who had connections with a great American foundation. Thoughts of what could happen to the cause of female education in Kenya if this foundation became interested, sent her thoughts, prayers, imagination, and faith soaring. She envisioned a great interdenominational school—a practical school that would finally change the whole course of Kenya's history. She remembered how she had achieved grants from the Government for the Bunyore Girls' School, and she decided to follow the same course. The God who had protected her from the Mau Mau would supply the money.

Her zeal for the new venture is indicated in the letters she mailed to her prayer-partners.

"Our place is buzzing with excitement as we are opening our exhibit and sale in Nairobi, November 15th. Each of our girls is trying her best to get her article finished. A few days ago I said, 'Girls, let's not talk and we will sew better.' A little Kikuyu girl, smiling from ear to ear, spoke up, 'Tell them the way to keep the Cup is to be quiet and win it again in 1958!' We took the Silver Cup away from a high school. There were fifty entries and we won first place over all the entries in Kenya."

She rejoiced in the cups her girls won because it gave them a thrilling success experience, proving that even though they were African girls they could do something really worthwhile. But her work did not end with sales. The sales were just a means to an end. At the close of this same letter she wrote: "God gave us a real shower of blessings not long ago—we had in our services forty-four seekers. I wish with all my heart that you who have been sending us funds and praying for us could have been there. Satan had to take a back seat! Oh, how he hates to see God's people capture the land!"

The year 1960 was an extremely difficult one. Father barely recovered from an illness—an illness the doctors had predicted would be fatal, and Mother had a very serious major operation. Besides this, there were many unusually vexing problems in the school. Some of the girls ran off, stealing their uniforms and whatever else they could lay their hands on. Funds became critically short. The native cry for *Uhuru* (Independence) was becoming more vocal, and thousands of white people began to stream from the Colony. But Mother took it all in her stride, for her eyes were on the stars. She remembered that the Southern Cross watched over Kenya. On November 16 she wrote:

"1960 has been a difficult year. We will put it away gladly, and by faith reach our hands to 1961. Let us keep our eyes on the great leader—the Christ. . . . Brother Ludwig and I are both well and busy, as we prepare for 1961. We need your prayers and cooperation. . . . Come, let us look at the task before us and do what we can to win out for God!"

On our copy of this printed letter, Mother wrote by hand: "This is now Christmas again—and we are thinking of you all, and hoping all is well with you. Each day we take you to the throne of grace. Why don't you spend a vacation with us?"

Four days later, she wrote again, putting the message down on the edge of the form letter. "We love you, each and every one and yearn to see you. Life is truly slipping away—and when it is too late we will wake up to realize that it is too late to see one another."

At this time she was unusually busy, getting ready for a great sale to start in the Memorial Hall on December 15. This sale was to be the best. Money just had to come in to pay the bills that were piling up. To each girl she said, "Now do your best. . . . Remember we are Christians, and only our best is good enough." The lights burned late at Ruarka as the sewing machines hummed, and the needles followed the outlines drawn for them. The girls sang as they worked.

In spite of the pressure of time, Mother thought of us and wrote: "I know you are busy getting your Christmas program ready. Oh, how I wish I were a little mouse and could crawl in the corner and watch. Pray for us. We're getting ready for the biggest sale we've ever had."

On December 14, Mother worked hard—seeing to every detail. She spoke to the girls as a general might speak to his troops. "We're building a New Africa with Christ. *We must do our best!*"

On December 15, she got up, poured herself a cup of tea from a pot with a cracked lid, and started getting everything ready to go into Nairobi for the sale. Then the doctor and health officer appeared to inspect the school. They hadn't been there for a long time, and Mother was thankful that they had come. She stuffed some more things into her nearly groaning pocketbook and waited. Then suddenly at 10:00 A.M. she became unconscious. Within two minutes the doctor was by her side and an ambulance was ordered.

She died in the New European Hospital that night at 7:55 P.M. The cause of her death was listed as a cerebral hemmorrhage. She didn't have a minute's warning.

The casket was carried to the grave by the husbands of her teachers. As they sloshed through the drenching rain the girls kept saying, "Mama isn't in that box. Mama is in heaven!" Dad was grief-stricken by the suddenness of the blow, but as the days went by he knew that this was the way Mother wanted things to be.

At the time of her death, she was in the middle of her seventieth year. I, of course, was unable to go to the funeral, but I called Father by long-distance telephone. The next day I expressed my feelings in our little church paper, *Contact:*

"Her body now lies in Africa where during the day the natives come and weep and pray and think of her work; and where at night when the hyenas and jackals are silent because of the roar of the lions, it is guarded by the light of the Southern Cross.

"Good night, Mother, good night. I'll see you in the morning!"